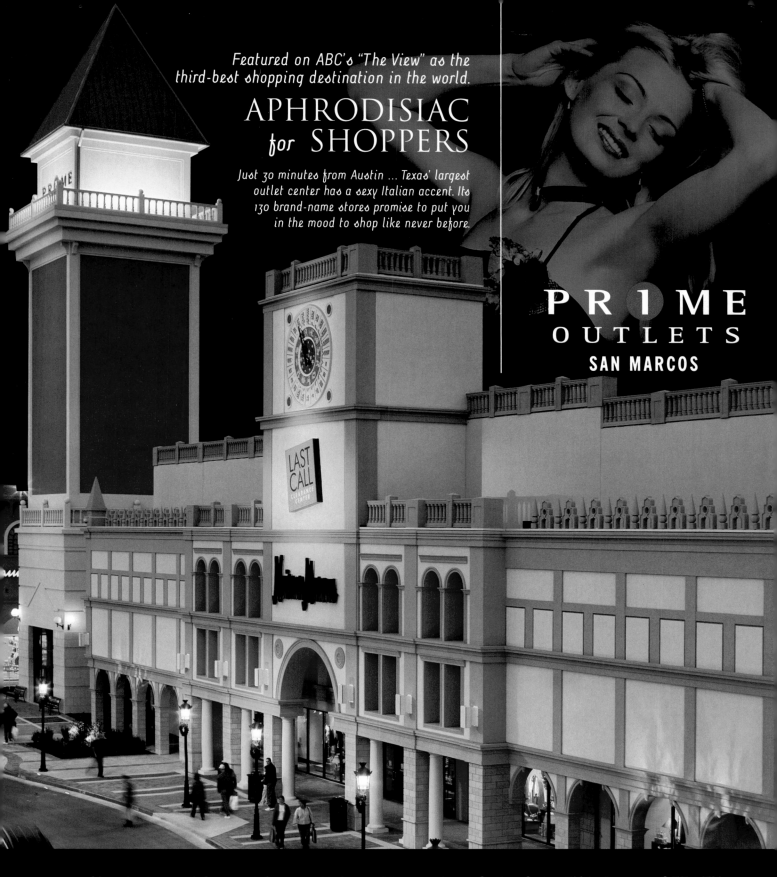

Featured on ABC's "The View" as the third-best shopping destination in the world.

APHRODISIAC *for* SHOPPERS

Just 30 minutes from Austin ... Texas' largest outlet center has a sexy Italian accent. Its 130 brand-name stores promise to put you in the mood to shop like never before.

PR1ME
OUTLETS
SAN MARCOS

Giorgio Armani General Store • Neiman Marcus Last Call • Saks Fifth Avenue OFF 5TH
Catherine Malandrino • La Perla • Salvatore Ferragamo Company Store • kate spade
Michael Kors • Lacoste Outlet • Zegna Outlet

IH-35 to Exit 200, Centerpoint Road, San Marcos • 800.628.9465 • primeoutlets.com

Schlitterbahn®
WATERPARK RESORT
New Braunfels, Texas

OPEN DAILY DURING THE SUMMER & WEEKENDS IN LATE APRIL, EARLY MAY & EARLY SEPTEMBER!

Schlitterbahn

Bring Your Own Picnic!

Just Minutes South of Austin!

schlitterbahn.com

World's Best Waterpark Is Just Minutes Away!

Less than an hour south of Austin, in the charming German community of New Braunfels, you'll find the waterpark named best in America! Schlitterbahn Waterpark Resort, a sprawling 65-acre celebration of water, has been named the number one waterpark by the Travel Channel.

It's the unique combination of a beautiful natural setting, small-town Texas hospitality and the greatest variety of water attractions anywhere that sets Schlitterbahn apart. Nestled along the banks of a spring-fed river, many of the park's rides use cool, spring water as they weave among century-old oak trees. And under those huge shade trees you'll find hundreds of picnic tables. That's right! You can bring your own picnic to Schlitterbahn if you wish. What other major theme park lets you do that? (Please no glass or alcohol.)

But it's the rides that have made Schlitterbahn famous around the world. Rides like the world's first surfing ride, tube chutes that stretch for miles, water playgrounds that delight the kids and water slides that blast you uphill! And with over 230 overnight accommodations, you can even stay right IN Schlitterbahn.

To get the complete Schlitterbahn story, visit our website at schlitterbahn.com or call 830-625-2351!

Schlitterbahn is open weekends from late April to late May, daily during the summer and weekends until mid-September. Resort accommodations are available year-round!

FREE PARKING   FREE INNER TUBES   BRING YOUR PICNIC
(no alcohol or glass please)

Two More Schlitterbahns! Two More Ways to Have Fun!

Located on the Gulf of Mexico in tropical South Padre Island, Schlitterbahn Beach Waterpark has a dozen state-of-the-art family rides plus the Shrimp Haus full-service restaurant with spectacular views. The waterpark is open seasonally while the restaurant is open year-round. 956.772.7873

The newest member of the Schlitterbahn family is located on historic Galveston Island. With the very latest and greatest ways to have fun in the water, Schlitterbahn Galveston Island Waterpark will thrill adults and children alike! The full waterpark is open during the summer season. Plus on most fall, winter and spring weekends you can enjoy the first heated, indoor waterpark in Texas at Wasserfest. For operating dates and times please visit www.schlitterbahn.com or call 409.770.9283.

your address
AUSTIN

making the city your home

Styling More
THAN JUST YOUR HOME

Now! Shop On-line at
WWW.YOURADDRESSMAGAZINE.COM

Subscribe On-line Today for Only $9.95

Thank you to our Holiday 2007 Features (from left) Jean Paul DeJoria and family, Todd Allen and family, Tyson Cox.

Estância Churrascaria

BRAZILIAN STEAK HOUSE

First Authentic Brazilian Steak House in Austin

For a set price you will enjoy an amazing salad bar with over 25 of the freshest ingredients like hearts of palm, asparagus, sun dried tomatoes, fresh mozzarella and much more! When guests are ready, our professional chefs will personally serve you at your table over 12 savory cuts of meat including beef, lamb, pork, chicken and sausage. Accompanying your meal will be traditional Brazilian side dishes of golden fried bananas, garlic mashed potatoes, polenta, rice and beans and our heavenly homemade cheese bread rolls, ENJOY!

Extensive Wine List and Full Bar

4894 Highway 290 West   Sunset Valley, TX 78735   (512) 892-1225
www.estanciachurrascaria.com

Lunch: Mon – Fri 11:00 AM – 2:00 PM Sat – Sun 11:30 AM – 3:00 PM
Dinner: Mon – Thu 5:00 PM – 10:00 PM Friday 5:00 – 10:30 PM
Saturday 4:00 PM – 10:30 PM Sunday 4:00 PM – 9:30 PM

STATE OF TEXAS
OFFICE OF THE GOVERNOR

As Governor, I am pleased to welcome you to Austin, the capital city of Texas. Whether you are from out of state or just out of town, *Celebrate Austin* will give you a good idea of what life is like in this most uncommon city.

Austin is a city of many different dimensions. Although it is the seat of state government, home to The University of Texas and an international center for the high-tech industry, Austin still has the cozy reputation as the Live Music Capital of the World. Add in the natural beauty of the highland lakes and the rolling Hill Country, the popular hike and bike trail along Town Lake, and you have a most unique setting for the typically laidback Austin lifestyle.

In Austin, you will find a thriving cultural life, celebrated by world-class events such as the Austin City Limits Music Festival and South by Southwest, to the typically quirky Austin celebrations of Eeyore's birthday party and Spamarama. The visual arts thrive against the rich cultural tapestry of Austin. The Blanton Museum displays modern and traditional art, while the Ransom Center houses one of the rare Gutenberg Bibles printed on his moveable type press. And most busy street corners house a street artisan or two.

Downtown Austin is an illuminating place of entertainment and enjoyment. The skyline is growing with more and more housing units that will augment the vitality of the center of the city. Venues such as the Zachary Scott Theatre and the Paramount Theater showcase the performing arts scene of Austin. And the local restaurants are not only enjoyable, but distinctive to the unique mixture of cultures that is Austin. No matter the time of day, there is always a restaurant to appease any hungry appetite.

I encourage visitors and residents alike to enjoy all our great city has to offer. There is surely something for everyone to participate in and truly capture the spirit of Austin

First Lady Anita Perry joins me in encouraging you to enjoy and explore Austin.

Sincerely

Rick Perry

Rick Perry
Governor

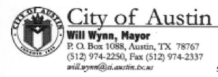
City of Austin
Will Wynn, Mayor
P. O. Box 1088, Austin, TX 78767
(512) 974-2250, Fax (512) 974-2337
will.wynn@ci.austin.tx.us

On behalf of the City of Austin, I would like to welcome you to the Capital City. We are proud to be the home if the University of Texas Longhorns, beautiful landscapes and some of the best entertainment, shopping and dining in the Lone Star State

Austin is a special place, but what makes it unique is hard to define. It's partly the people – a richly diverse mix of students and tech millionaires, artists and engineers, musicians and entrepreneurs, small-business men and women. It's partly our cultural scene, earning us the reputation as the Live Music Capital of the World, but that only skims the surface of the arts and entertainment available here. Ultimately it's the indefinable qualities that make Austin magical.

During your stay, I invite you to explore the many landmarks and museums that have made Austin one of the most dynamic cities in the country. The Texas State Capitol is a popular tourist attraction and a favorite spot for Austinites. Other points of interest include the Governor's Mansion, the Blanton Museum of Art and the Bob Bullock Texas State History Museum.

Enjoy your stay in Austin, and we hope you visit us again soon.

Regards,

Will Wynn

Will Wynn
Mayor

Celebrate Staf

PRESIDENT & PUBLISHER
Judy Barrick

EXECUTIVE VICE PRESIDENT
Linda Olson
Marilyn Crawford

EDITOR
Kelly Ayoub

ACCOUNTANT
Claire Costin

ART DIRECTOR
Shannon Skinto

ASSISTANT ART DIRECTOR
Tyler Lee

DESIGN ASSISTANT
Megan Klein

SENIOR SALES EXECUTIVE
Meagan Staff

ACCOUNT EXECUTIVE
Erin Gold

COVER PHOTOGRAPHER
Randy Smith

PHOTOGRAPHERS
Nick Simonite
L. Andrew Sterling
Winker

WEB DESIGN
Nick DeBellas
Kristian Oubre

CONTRIBUTING WRITERS
James Bridges
Christine Cha-Sartori
Kathryn Cleland
Cara Henis
Libby Dean Hope
Jennifer Jurenak
Stephanie Matlock
Christine Pham
Brandon Renner
Whitney Priddy
Saralee Tiede

ADVERTISING INQUIRIES
publisher@celebrateaustin.cor

JOB AND INTERNSHIP INQUIRI
jobs@celebrateaustin.com

Celebrate Austin (ISBN 1-893524-20-9
Celebrate Horseshoe Bay (ISBN 1-89352
22-1) and Celebrate Marble Falls (ISBN
1-89352-21-3) are published by Celebrat
Texas Publications, Inc. Corporate office
are located at 10713 RR 620 N, Austin, Te
78726. For advertising information, please
512-346-6235.

2ND STREET DISTRICT

40+ Specialty Retailers & Restaurants
GEMS TO GELATO
ANY COMBINATION. ONE DESTINATION.

SHOP

Area Furniture
117 Lavaca
512-474-2732
Contemporary & antique furnishings

Cathy's Cleaners
231 West 3rd Street
cathyscleaners.net
512-320-8111
Cleaners and alterations

Cowboy Cool
217 West 2nd Street
cowboycool.com
512-708-9000
Western gear with a contemporary edge

Design Within Reach
200 West 2nd Street
dwr.com
512-472-7200
Current & classic modern furniture

Eliza Page
229 West 2nd Street
elizapage.com
512-474-6500
Innovative designer fine jewelry

Estilo
234 West 2nd Street
estiloaustin.com
512-236-0488
A contemporary clothing gallery

Finch
417 West 2nd Street
shopfinch.com
512-236-1414
Gifts & accessories for the home

Girl Next Door
250 West 2nd Street
girlnd.com
512-322-0501
An Austin shopping experience
for women

IF + Design
208 Colorado Street
ifdaustin.com
512-469-0870
Furniture, flooring, local art + design

LOFT
416 Cesar Chavez
lofthomedecor.com
512-377-6810
Furniture, gifts, accessories & more

Lofty Dog
403 West 2nd Street
austinloftydog.com
512-476-5050
Pet products & accessories
for the urban dog

Mercury Design Studio
209 West 2nd Street
mercurydesignstudio.com
512-236-0100
Vintage style, modern living

Milk and Honey Day Spa
204 Colorado Street
milkandhoneyspa.com
512-236-1115
Austin's premier day spa

Mototek
241 West 3rd Street
mototek.com
512-236-8822
Aprilia & Ducati scooters
& motorcycles

Octane
201 West 2nd Street
myoctane.com
214-219-3118
Designer denim and
clothing boutique

Peyton's Place
215 Lavaca Street
512-477-5223
Casual contemporary
women's clothing

Sana
237 West 2nd Street
sana-austin.com
512-801-5858
Sophisticated women's
clothing boutique

Shiki
225 West 2nd Street
shikistyle.com
512-391-0123
Contemporary women's
clothing boutique

Shorelines Gallery
221 West 2nd Street
shorelinesgalleryaustin.com
512-322-9661
Fine art & designer jewelry

St. Bernard Sports
401 W. 3rd Street
stbernardsports.com
512-320-1999
Sportswear & gear

The Home Retreat
249 West 2nd Street
thehomeretreat.com
512-391-0330
Fine home linens & décor

Wee
417 1/2 West 2nd Street
www.shopwee.com
512-236-1338
COMING SOON

DINE

III Forks
111 Lavaca Street
iiiforks.com
512-474-1776
A find dining steakhouse

Austin Java City Hall Cafe
301 West 2nd Street
austinjava.com
512-481-9400
Breakfast, lunch, dinner & desserts

Cantina Laredo
201 West 3rd Street
cantinalaredo.com
512-542-9670
Gourmet Mexican food

CRU Wine Bar
238 West 2nd Street
cruawinebar.com
512-472-9463
Austin's premier wine bar

Jo's Hot Coffee
242 West 2nd Street
joscoffee.com
512-444-3800
...and good food, cold beer
& live music

Lambert's BBQ
401 West 2nd Street
lambertsaustin.com
512-494-1500
Modern interpretations
of Texas cuisine

Leaf
419 West 2nd Street
leafsalad.com
512-474-LEAF(5323)
The place for a great salad

Malaga
248 W. 2nd Street
malagatapasbar.com
COMING SOON

Mama Fu's
100 Colorado Street
mamafus.com
COMING SOON

Paciugo
241 West 2nd Street
paciugo.com
512-474-7600
Authentic Italian ice cream & cafè

Royal Blue Grocery
247 West 3rd Street
royalbluegrocery.com
512-499-3993
Downtown's neighborhood grocery

Sushi Sake
206 Colorado Street
sushisake.com
512-527-0888
Fine Japanese cuisine

Taste Select Wines
202 W. Cesar Chavez
512-284-9802
World-class wine shop &
tasting venue

Taverna
258 West 2nd Street
512-477-1001
Authentic Italian fare & cutting-
edge cuisine

Which Wich?
259 West 3rd Street
whichwich.com
512-472-WICH (9424)
Superior customized hot
sandwiches

Located in the heart of downtown Austin
www.2NDStreetDistrict.com

INSIDE
CELEBRATE AUSTIN

LIFESTYLE
15. Living Life to its Fullest
16. A Tribute to Lady Bird Johnson
18. Top 5 Ways to Live Like an Austinite
20. Event Calendar
21-22. Things to Do and See in Austin
   LAKE TRAVIS
23-27. The OASIS, Even Bigger and Better
28. Comanche Canyon Ranch
30. Top 5 Ways to Enjoy Beautiful Lake Travis

SPORTS-OUTDOORS
33. Austin's Active Side
34. Top 5 Ways to Stay Cool in the Texas Sun
36. Austin's Backyard

ARTS
39. Indulging in Austin's Artistic Side
40. Top 5 Reasons to Explore Austin's Art Scene
42. GALLERY MENU
43. Find it in the West End

LEISURE
45. Relax and Be Zen- It's Austin!
46. Top 5 Reasons Austin is the Best Place to Relax
47. Spa Etiquette, 5 Great Tips
47. SPA MENU
48. Community Spotlight, Pamela Brewer
49. A Day Off

CONCIERGE
51. Getting the Goods In Austin
52. Top 5 Ways to Make the Most of Your Stay
52. The Art of Giving Flowers
54. Traveler's Tipping Guide
55. The Keeper of the Keys

BUSINESS
57. Austin At Work
58. Top 5 Ways to Work in Austin
58. Next Stop: Silicon Hills

ENTERTAINMENT
63. A Night on the Town
64. Top 5 Ways to Enjoy Austin at Night
65. BAR MENU
66. Sixth Street Revealed
68. Saxon Pub Shares a Few Austin Memories

DINING
75. The Special Taste of Austin
76. Top 5 Local Beverages you Should Try
80. Market Fresh
82. Ciao Down!
84, 86, 88. DINING MENU

SHOPPING
91. Chic Shopping in Austin
93. Top 5 Places to Shop 'Til you Drop
102. Experience the Ultimate in Jewelry, Buckles &
104. A Midtown Oasis, 26 Doors Shopping Center

DESTINATIONS
109. When you Feel the Need to Get Away
110. Top 5 Incentives to Take a Day Trip
111. Don't Forget! Traveling Essentials

M-1 MARBLE FALLS
H-1 HORSESHOE BAY

Celebrate
Living Life to its Fullest

The lifestyle in Austin is truly different from any other city in the world. Visitors often ask the question, "What makes Austin so weird...?"

BY JENNIFER JURANEK

The lifestyle in Austin is truly different from any other city in the world. Visitors often ask the question, "What makes Austin so weird or unique?" The great thing about Austin is the variety of answers. From housing the capitol building and Texas politics to the abundance of live music venues or the casual dress and atmosphere, people enjoy living in Austin for so many reasons.

One simple reason Austinites love their city is the environment. The breathtaking Texas Hill Country and almost yearlong sunshine make everyone here eager to enjoy the beauty of the outdoors. Luckily for Austinites, the city has endless ways to do so. Austin has an abundance of hike and bike trails, outdoor sports locations, and swimming holes. From gazing at the downtown skyline from a kayak on Town Lake to hiking past rock structures on the Greenbelt to sitting on an outdoor patio café near one of Austin's lakes, the idea remains the same: the prestine beauty of Austin is one to be enjoyed.

Although Austin has many places to slow down, relax, and enjoy life, the business and technology industries also thrive here. The prestigious schools and universities, including the University of Texas and St. Edward's, provide students from across the country with a chance to get an education, form new ideas, and change the world for the better.

The most boasted title Austin holds is "The Live Music Capital of the World." Home to famous music events such as the Austin City Limits Music Festival and South by Southwest, many famous musicians flock to Austin to showcase their talent, bringing music buffs along to enjoy it. However, often unknown local musicians put on the most heartfelt shows, and with its abundance of live music venues, Austin is an oasis for these up and coming musicians. Whether celebrating rock's roots at a local blues club or dancing to country music in cowboy boots, Austinites can enjoy music from any genre on any day of the week.

There are many advantages to living in Austin, including the hip shops, the lovely scenery, the cooperative weather and the incomperable music. But there is an unspoken, more intangible reason that Austin is such an amazing place to live. Something about the unique spirit of Austin makes it relaxed yet chic. In Austin, business executives, activists, sports enthusiasts, music lovers, cowboys and students comfortably mix and mingle on Guadalupe Street or listening to music on Sixth Street. It is this unique blend of different types of people that makes every facet of life in Austin so special.

Lady Bird Johnson

BY SARALEE TIEDE 1912 - 2007

WIFE, MOTHER, GRANDMOTHER, CONSERVATIONIST, BUSINESSWOMAN, PHILANTHROPIST, FIRST LADY. LADY BIRD JOHNSON HOLDS CLAIM TO ALL OF THOSE TITLES AND MORE.

All her life, Mrs. Johnson has brought beauty to her sprawling family, to the Texas Hill Country she loves, and to the nation that loves her.

She inspired the passage of the Beautification Act of 1965—a bill her husband called a "gift" to his wife—which cemented environmentalism as a top priority in the United States. Married for four decades to one of the most powerful men in the world, Mrs. Johnson juggled extraordinarily demanding jobs as her husband's closest advisor as he rose from Congressman to Senator to Vice President to President and as mother to daughters Lynda Bird and Luci Baines. After her husband's death, she spent the next three and a half decades solidifying all that she had laid in place during their marriage.

Today, Lady Bird Johnson's legacy lives on in the millions of blooms planted in the nation's capital, in the sweeping banks of wildflowers lining U.S. highways, and in the charm of Austin's revitalized Town Lake. An equally lasting legacy is her extraordinary family—Lynda Johnson Robb and her husband Charles; Luci Baines Johnson and her husband Ian Turpin; six granddaughters and one grandson; and 10 great-grandchildren.

Mrs. Johnson was born Claudia Alta Taylor in the East Texas town of Karnack on December 22, 1912. Her father, Thomas Jefferson Taylor, was owner of a general store. Her mother, Minnie Pattillo Taylor, died when Claudia was five years old, leaving the little girl and her two older brothers, Tommy and Tony, in the care of their father and their Aunt Effie. Legend has it that a nursemaid said Claudia was "as purty as a lady bird"; the sweet nickname suited her and stuck for life.

Mrs. Johnson graduated from Marshall High School in 1928 and attended Saint Mary's Episcopal School for Girls in Dallas from 1928 to 1930. She then entered The University of Texas at Austin, graduating in 1933 with a Bachelor of Arts in History and in 1934, with a Bachelor of Journalism with honors.

She met the tall, ambitious man whom she would marry when he was a Congressional secretary visiting Austin on official business. Lyndon Baines Johnson courted Lady Bird Taylor with all the single-minded energy he would later bring to elected office. They were engaged just seven weeks after their first date and married in November 1934.

Mrs. Johnson recalled that "sometimes Lyndon simply [took] your breath away." Her life with Lyndon Johnson was one of such achievements in politics, business and philanthropy; it left those around them breathless, too.

Lady Bird Johnson is probably best known for her support of her husband's career. When Lyndon Johnson volunteered for the U.S. Navy in World War II, Mrs. Johnson ran his Congressional office, serving constituents' needs in every way except voting. Her support for her husband's political career continued throughout his years in government. She campaigned actively for his race for the Congress, Senate, vice presidency and presidency. In 1960, she covered 35,000 miles for the Kennedy/Johnson ticket, and in 1964, she campaigned independently on a whistle-stop train throughout the South for the Johnson/Humphrey ticket. President Johnson paid her the highest of compliments, saying he thought that the voters "would happily have supported her over me."

Lady Bird Johnson stood by her husband on the fateful November day in 1963 when Lyndon Johnson became the 36th President of the United States after the assassination of John Kennedy. Her official White House biography notes that her gracious personality and Texas hospitality did much to heal the pain of those dark days. She created a First Lady's Committee for a More Beautiful Capital and then expanded her program to include the entire nation. She was also highly involved in the President's War on Poverty, focusing in particular on Project Head Start for preschool children.

While President Johnson was still in office, Mrs. Johnson played a key role in the plans to build the LBJ Library and Museum and the LBJ School of Public Affairs in Austin, Texas. The Library is in the process of building the Lady Bird Johnson Center, consisting of educational classrooms and outdoor landscaping. After the Johnsons' White House years ended in 1969, Mrs. Johnson authored *A White House Diary*, a memoir that drew on her considerable skills as a writer and historian. "I was keenly aware that I had a unique opportunity, a front row seat, on an unfolding story and nobody else was going to see it from quite the vantage point that I saw it." She also co-authored *Wildflowers Across America* with Carlton Lees. In December 1972, President and Mrs. Johnson gave the LBJ Ranch house and surrounding property to the people of the United States as a national historic site.

On her 70th birthday in 1982, Mrs. Johnson founded the National Wildflower Research Center, a nonprofit environmental organization dedicated to the preservation and re-establishment of native plants in natural and planned landscapes. She donated funding and 60 acres of land in Austin to establish the organization. In December 1997, the property was renamed the Lady Bird Johnson Wildflower Center in honor of Mrs. Johnson's 85th birthday. In 2006, the Lady Bird Johnson Wildflower Center became a part of The University of Texas at Austin, guaranteeing its permanent place in the national landscape—and ensuring that Lady Bird Johnson's name will live on in the hearts of Americans.

Are you an Entrepreneur at Heart?

Feel Like Escaping The Corporate Constraints?

Join the Publishing World as an Associate Publisher and Take Charge of your Life!

Take the leadership position as an Associate Publisher for Your Address Magazine in your city.
Offer your neighbors the opportunity to enjoy a gorgeous, high-gloss home and lifestyle magazine
that features relevant and compelling editorial and provides your advertisers with a venue to
showcase their products and services.
We deliver unrivaled distribution, incredible graphics and solid returns for the advertisers.

Earning potential is unlimited - a dedicated entrepreneur has unlimited earning potential. Earn the money you want and have the time to enjoy it!

Receive a proven turnkey system. Publishing a magazine is a complex business that requires creative talent and many years of experience.
Our turnkey system allows the energetic and enthusiastic Associate Publisher, eager to greet each day, an opportunity to build a successful business.

Your Address Magazine is expanding nationwide.
Make a choice to own *Your Address Magazine* in your city – become an Associate Publisher TODAY!

To learn more visit us on the web at www.youraddressmagazine.com, email associatepublisher@youraddressmagazine.com or call 512-371-7171

Top 5 Ways to Live Like an Austinite

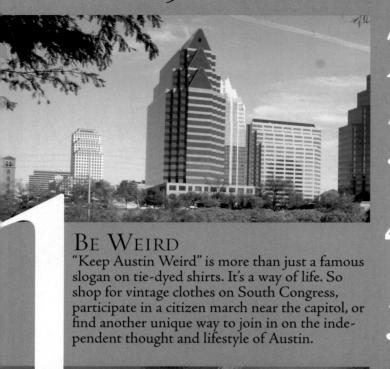

1 Be Weird

"Keep Austin Weird" is more than just a famous slogan on tie-dyed shirts. It's a way of life. So shop for vintage clothes on South Congress, participate in a citizen march near the capitol, or find another unique way to join in on the independent thought and lifestyle of Austin.

2 Be Healthy

Austin is known for its variety of health food options, such as fresh food markets and numerous Co-op groceries. Whether visiting one of the many local vegetarian a vegan restaurants or relaxing at a yoga studio, there are many ways to join the well-balanced Austin lifestyle.

3 Get Outside

Austin is proud to be the home of numerous parks, hik and bike trails, lakes, and swimming holes. Pair these diverse recreational locations with almost yearlong war weather and sunshine, and you have Austin: an amazin city to celebrate the beauty of the outdoors.

4 Learn Something New

Austin has numerous top rated universities, making it a wonderful place to get a formal education. However, it doesn't end there; Austin also has many museums, libraries, galleries, centers for politics, and various othe places to create your own informal education.

5 Have Fun

Austin is known for its annual festivals, parties, and places to kick-back, relax and enjoy life. Go fly a kite at the Zilker Park, enjoy Tex-Mex at a local Austin restau rant or dance to country music at a live music venue on Sixth Street to make the most of your time here!

Calendar of Events

JANUARY

17-20, AUSTIN BOAT SHOW
Austin Convention Center;
500 East Cesar Chavez, Austin,
TX 78701; 512-494-1128; www.
austinboatshow.com

18-20, CUSTOM CAR & HOT ROD
SHOW; Parmer Events Center;
www.austincarshow.com

21, MARTIN LUTHER KING JR.
FESTIVAL
Hutson Tillotson University;
900 Chicon Street, Austin,
TX 78702; 512-505-3306;
www.mlkcelebration.com/
marchandrally.php

FEBRUARY

2, CARNAVAL BRASILEIRO
Palmer Events Center; 900
Barton Springs Road, Austin, TX
78704; 512-219-1292;
www.sambaparty.com

29 - MARCH 15, STAR OF TEXAS
FAIR AND RODEO;
www.rodeoaustin.com

MARCH

1, EXPLORE UT
The University of Texas; Austin,
TX 78712; www.utexas.edu/
events/exploreut

7-16, SOUTH BY SOUTHWEST
INTERACTIVE MUSIC AND FILM
FESTIVALS
512-467-7979; www.sxsw.com

29, LOUISIANA SWAMP THING
AND CRAWFISH FESTIVAL
www.roadstarproductions.com

APRIL

10-13, 23RD ANNUAL TEXAS HILL
COUNTRY WINE AND FOOD
FESTIVAL 512-249-6300;
www.texaswineandfood.org

12-13, MUSTER DAY : A
CELEBRATION OF TEXAS MILITARY
HISTORY
512-782-5770;
www.texasmilitaryforcesmuseum.
org

26, EEYORE'S 45TH ANNUAL
BIRTHDAY PARTY
Pease Park; 1100 Kingsbury
Street, Austin, TX 78703; 512-
448-5160; eeyores.sexton.com

MAY

3-4, OLD PECAN STREET SPRING
FESTIVAL
6th Street from I-35 to Brazos,
and on 7th Street from Trinity to
Red River; 512-443-6179; www.
oldpecanstreetfestival.com

23-26, REPUBLIC OF TEXAS BIKER
RALLY
Travis County Exposition Center;
7311 Decker Lane, Austin, TX
78724; 214-705-1036; www.
rotrally.com

24-26, AUSTIN WINE FESTIVAL
www.austinwinefestival.com

JUNE

14, KEEP AUSTIN WEIRD 5K AND
MUSIC FESTIVAL
Republic Square Park; 422
Guadalupe, Austin, TX 78701;
www.keepaustinweirdfest.com

JULY

4, H-E-B AUSTIN SYMPHONY
JULY 4TH FIREWORKS
Lady Bird Lake. Auditorium
Shores at the Long Center; 501
Congress Avenue, Austin, TX
78701; www.austinsymphony.org

AUGUST

AUSTN CHRONICLE HOT SAUCE
FESTIVAL WATERLOO PARK; www.
austinchronicle.com; date TBD

2ND ANNUAL AUSTIN ICE CREAM
FESTIVAL
Waterloo Park; 1301 Trinity
Street, Austin, TX 78701; 512-
923-1726; date TBD
www.icecreamfestival.org

SEPTEMBER

14-16 AUSTIN CITY LIMITS
MUSIC FESTIVAL
Zilker Metropolitan Park; 2100
Barton Springs Road, Austin, TX
78746; www.aclfestival.com

15, DIEZ Y SEIS CELEBRATION
www.ci.austin.tx.us/parks/
diezyseis.htm

OCTOBER

27, DIA DE LOS MUERTOS
Mexic-Arte Museum; www.
mexic-artemuseum.com

31, HALLOWEEN ON SIXTH STREET
East Sixth Street, Austin TX;
www.6street.com

NOVEMBER

1, AUSTIN POWWOW AND
AMERICAN INDIAN HERITAGE
FESTIVAL
512-371-0628; www.
austinpowwow.org

DECEMBER

5-7 & 12-14, HOLIDAY WINE
TRAIL
www.texaswinetrail.com

7, ZILKER PARK TREE LIGHTING
Zilker Metropolitan Park; 2100
Barton Springs Road, Austin,
TX 78746; 512-974-6700; www.
ci.austin.tx.us/tol/tree

FOR MORE UPDATED AND CURRENT EVENTS IN THE EXCITING CITY OF AUSTIN, TEXAS,
PLEASE VISIT OUR WEBSITE AT WWW.CELEBRATEAUSTIN.COM!

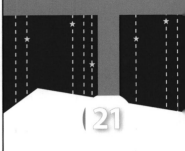

AUSTIN IS A FABULOUS CITY IN WHICH TO FIND AMAZING AND UNIQUE ATTRACTIONS AND SHOPS. WE INVITE YOU TO EXPLORE THESE LOCAL AUSTIN FINDS THAT WILL MAKE YOUR TRIP SIMPLY UNFORGETTABLE. WHETHER YOU ARE TAKING A TOUR, EXPLORING A MUSEUM OR SHOPPING FOR SOUVENIRS, OUR SPECIAL RECOMMENDATIONS ARE SURE TO PLEASE!

AIRSCAPE PARASAIL

Fly high above Lake Travis for the thrill and the view. Take off and landing is on the boat's deck, so parasailing is fun for all ages anytime of the year! Fly alone or double. Great special occasion celebration, gift certificates available. Pick up available from various locations. 512-257-9675; www.airscapeparasail.com

ARABIC BAZAAR

Directly imports beautiful treasures from Syria, Egypt and Morocco. Selections include jewelry, rugs, furniture, antiques, lamps, brass and glassware, leather goods, mosaic boxes, Egyptian hookas, belly dance costumes, clothing, perfume oils, cosmetics and soaps. Custom design and shipping available. Arabic Bazaar; 5013 Duval St.; 512-533-9227; www.wmdproductions.com

ELECTRIC CARS OF AUSTIN

Looking for an alternative to the skyrocketing gas prices? Or a trendy car to jet around in? Electric cars for sale have just rolled into Austin with the first dealership now open, marking the beginning of new transportation options for motorists. Electric Cars of Austin; 704 N. Lamar Blvd.; 512-472-4222; www.electriccarsofaustin.com

LBJ WILDFLOWER CENTER

Enjoy the gardens, nature trails (including a wheelchair-accessible research trail), Wild Ideas: The Store, Wildflower Café, tours and children's programs at the 279-acre Wildflower Center. Open Tuesday-Saturday 9:00 am to 5:30 pm. 4801 La Crosse Ave.; 512-292-4200; www.wildflower.org

LONE STAR RIVERBOATS

Enjoy a Texas-friendly public sightseeing or Sunset Bat-Watching cruise aboard the Lone Star or Little Star on beautiful Town Lake. Reservations recommended. Private charters, full catering and beverage service also available. When you ride Lone Star Riverboat, a portion of all sales helps support Austin's parks. Family-owned and operated. 512-327-1388; www.lonestarriverboats.com

AUSTIN DUCK ADVENTURES

For a unique tour of downtown, hop on-board this amphibious vehicle that travels the city streets before splashing into Lake Austin. Tours depart daily from the Austin Visitor's Center. 1605 W 5th Street Austin, TX 78703; 512- 477-5274; www.austinducks.com

AUSTIN CARRIAGE SERVICES

Tours, wedding transportation, leisure rides and pick up/drop off downtown. Make reservations four hours in advance. Mention Celebrate Austin for a discount. Weeknights, dusk to 11pm and weekend nights, dusk to 1am. **Standard service for six: $40/30 min., $60/45 min., or $80/1 hour (before discounts).** 512-243-0044, www.austincarriage.com

BOBALU

Got Cubans? Watch authentic Cuban cigar rollers and enjoy the best Cuban coffee in Austin's only indoor smoking establishment on Sixth. Experience the finest cigars north of Havana. Custom-labeled and flavored cigars, lighters, accessories. Open daily. Highly recommended! 509 E 6th St., 512-469-5877; 888-33CIGAR, www.livecigarrollers.com

LUCKY LIZARD/ MUSEUM OF THE WEIRD

In the heart of Austin's famous 6th Street lies the city's most curious and mysterious gift shop, featuring an intriguing blend of local art, imported goods, jewelry, and unusual one-of-a-kind items and, of course, lizards! Featuring the Museum of the Weird-a must-see experience for visitors! 412 E. 6th St.; 512-476-5493; www.luckylizard.net

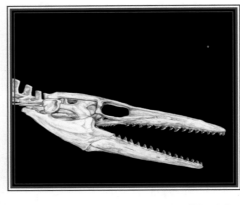

TEXAS MEMORIAL MUSEUM

Enjoy exhibits featuring dinosaurs, fossils, gems, minerals, and Texas wildlife. Visit our working paleontology lab and our impressive 3D visualization facility showing images of fossils scanned in UT's state-of-the-art CT scanner lab. 2400 Trinity Street ; 512-471-1604; www.utexas.edu/tmm

ZINGER HARDWARE

Locals declare, "It's a Zinga!" Relive your childhood in this store loaded with the coolest new gadgets, retro gifts, groovy glassware and furniture from around the world. Peruse the extensive line of Texas jams, salsas and BBQ sauces. Shipping available. 2438 W. Anderson Lane ; 512-533-9001; www.zingerhardware.com

The NEW OASIS

The
OASIS
Lake Travis

Celebrate
Lake Travis

THE BREATHTAKING VIEW FROM THE DECKS OF THE OASIS

The OASIS
Even Bigger and Better

Although devastated by a lightning induced fire June 1, 2005, The OASIS never faltered and is alive and has risen gloriously from the ashes. After the fire, owner Beau Theriot vowed The OASIS would be rebuilt even bigger and better than before.... he kept his word. The environment of The Oasis restaurant makes it a welcome place for celebration. When the sun sets, a bell is rung and the ending of the day is celebrated with applause. The restaurant seems to draw each customer into a different realm of nature and beauty. Originally loved as a unique overgrown tree house, hanging on the dramatic cliffs above Lake Travis, The OASIS offered the most spectacular sunsets in Texas. The new OASIS captures all that and more (*see photo, right*).

As well as the familiar decks and outdoor bars welcoming you with the "Perfect Margarita", there are now two floors of comfortable dining areas in the main restaurant for your year-round enjoyment. The third floor with its

pular entertainment area, Starlight, comes to life
an exceptional entertainment venue. When the
ique roll back roof is in play you will immediately
ow why it's named Starlight as you gaze up to the
avenly Texas night sky. Famous for its use of
ustin's world-class music talent, Starlight is truly
place for all to enjoy.

To the local Austin area, the Event
enter at The OASIS has become a landmark
r special occasions, from weddings, anniversary
ebrations, Bar and Bat Mitzvahs, to graduation
rties and corporate events. The flagship in
e fleet of private rooms, the casually elegant
p of The OASIS is the perfect setting for a
ecial evening high above Lake Travis. The
w configuration of the second floor allows for
xibility, comfortably accommodating groups of
00 to 1,200 for enjoyment of all the new decks
d spectacular views. Any occasion that requires
touch of class would be perfectly suited to these
enic rooms with the magnificent view of the lake
d the surrounding hill country.

Many Austinites consider The OASIS
ne of the most romantic sites for a special outing
d most certainly one of the best ways to enjoy any
y. The combination of the lake and sunset create
memorable atmosphere that is both treasured and
ared. It has become a popular tourist spot named
The Austin American Statesman as one of Texas'
p ten tourist attractions and draws people from
over the world to enjoy its ambiance. Theriot's
n words perhaps capture best the amazing allure
The OASIS: "I've been all over the world and
ve visited some gorgeous spots. But this place
ins my vote as the most fabulous I've ever seen
imagine finding this view in Texas!"

And Austinites are ever so glad that he
d.

The OASIS Restaurant is located at
550 Comanche Trail. Please call 512.266.2442 or
sit www.oasis-austin.com.

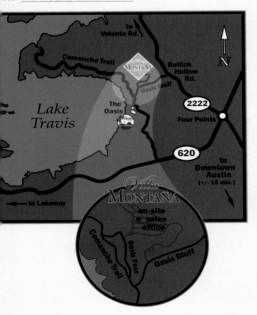

A UNIQUE SHOPPING EXPERIENCE COMING TO LAKE TRAVIS, AUSTIN... OASIS, TEXAS.

An innovative and unique shopping village is in the planning stages to share the spectacular cliff-top view of Lake Travis alongside the legendary OASIS restaurant. Recognizing that Austinites, Texans from other parts of the state and travelers from around the world have come to revere this exquisite lakeside vantage point with its heart-of-Texas feel as almost sacred ground, the creators of this project are designing this new addition to honor all that the OASIS has come to mean to its devotees from near and far. The eclectic nature of the beloved OASIS will set the tone for the environmentally sensitive approach to the creation of the village.

The owners of the venture are collaborating with local architect Dick Clark to plan the village, which will feature natural local stones and woods that will be incorporated into the design of every building in the center – each of which will have its own distinct, individual character. Outdoor sculpture gardens created by local artists, water falls, grottos and scenic outlooks will be yours to discover as you stroll along winding walkways with an old-world feel among a variety of one-of-a-kind shops, most of which will be boutiques and restaurants home grown in the Austin area and featuring products created locally.

The owners will take a sustainable or "green" approach to building the project, using recycled materials and environmentally sensitive building practices. They will also strive to achieve LEEDS Platinum certification for sustainable building. Some of the features will include a water tower which will capture rainwater to be filtered and used for irrigation, way-finding lighting powered by solar energy and locally supplied materials and landscaping elements that will reduce the environmental impact from shipping non-local supplies to the site.

The builders are also planning a world-class spa and fitness center along with limited office space designed to complement the Villa Montaña and surrounding residences. The design of the entire project will blend seamlessly with the surrounding bird preserve and highlight one of the most spectacular and inspiring views in this part of the world. Construction to begin early 2008.

"THE INTERIOR PIAZZA AND THE SPANISH STEPS"

Comanche Canyon Ranch

Villa Montaña and mirasol, Jewels Nestled in the Hills Above Lake Travis

Comanche Canyon Ranch
REALTY

Comanche Canyon Ranch provides a peaceful refuge just twenty minutes from the state capital. With beautiful Lake Travis and Hill Country vistas, it encompasses 448 acres. The OASIS owner Beau Theriot has held this prime Lake Travis real estate privately for over 28 years and has recently embarked on developing a limited number of unique settings for home, condos, specialty office and retail spaces. It was always a dream of Theriot's to have a place that would remain just as nature intended it. Even now, as the property is being developed, three-fourths of the land is set aside as a bird sanctuary and nature preserve, providing park-like and lush settings for the exclusive neighborhood.

The first residential neighborhood jewel - *Villa Montaña*, (www.villamontanatexas.com) is a gated community, that reflects a quiet ambiance of serenity in a variety of settings, offering only 98 lots and custom homes with spectacular lake and sunset views, lush canyon vistas and uniquely intimate garden style villas. Offering on-property concierge services for homeowners, all underground utilities, elegant landscaping weaving its way among the homes; along with antique style lanterns aligning pedestrian walkways, all create this majestic hillside village

– a rare opportunity for the most discriminating buyers. New residents are already enjoying their new paradise.

Mirasol, the second and newest jewel within Comanche Canyon Ranch is an upscale, eco-friendly residential community featuring 30 single-family lots. It is located across the street from the legendary Oasis restaurant. *Mirasol* (www.mirasollaketravis.com) provides Austin buyers with high-end new homes built in the OASIS' neighborhood. Mangum Builders will be spearheading the project. Lots are currently available for sale. Also a closed gated community, all of the home sites are nestled on a bluff surrounded by a nature preserve with some having Lake Travis views. Homes will be similar to developer Beau Theriot's adjacent *Villa Montaña*, with controlled architectural guidelines and premium building materials, using stone and stucco exteriors, windows, doors tile roofs, courtyards, and green materials used extensively.

Both communities offer an inspiring fusion of cutting edge architecture and environmental principle in an exceptional neighborhood setting, creating an inviting European Mediterranean ambiance.

Sales and marketing by Comanche Canyon Ranch Realty (www.ccranchrealty.com) located on-site. Please call 512.535.4667 or 512.266.4930 for more information.

ALSO WITHIN COMANCHE CANYON RANCH:
Shopping for furniture and art is always a beautiful adventure at THE TREASURY. SHOWCASING UNIQUE ANTIQUES, SOFT MODERN FURNISHINGS FOR YOUR HOME, OFFICE OR RANCH AND QUALITY DECORATIVE ACCESSORIES FOR ALL LIFESTYLES, THE TREASURY OFFERS INTERIOR DESIGN SERVICES AS WELL. LOCATED ACROSS THE STREET FROM THE OASIS, IT IS AN EASY WALK FOR RELAXED AND UNIQUE SHOPPING. 6535 COMANCHE TRAIL, 512.266.6444.

Top 5 Ways to Enjoy Beautiful Lake Travis

PHOTO COURTESY OF THE OASIS

1 SAIL AWAY

Lake Travis is home to many marinas and boating organizations that organize sailing activities all year long. There are races to enjoy most weekends and weekday evenings during the summer. The annual regattas hosted by the Austin Yacht Club with gorgeous sails on parade are truly a sight to behold.

2 TAKE A DIVE

With its crystal clear waters, Lake Travis attracts divers from all around to marvel at the wildlife and unique geographical formations found deep within. Master Scuba instructors in the area offer training classes and guided dives for beginners and advanced divers alike.

3 GO FISHING

Chock full of bass, bluegills, catfish, drum, sunfish and trout, Lake Travis is sure to satisfy even the most discriminating anglers. The more than 270 miles of shoreline cradle rock bluffs that are ideal for bringing in a big catch. In the spring and fall, the area's peak fishing seasons, it is common to bring in 20-30 bass a day!

4 GET CAMPY

Numerous public parks, maintained by either the Lower Colorado River Authority (LCRA) or Travis County, offer comfortable camping grounds complete with swimming holes, boat ramps, barbeque pits, hiking trails, picnic areas and restroom facilities.

5 GET BACK TO NATURE

It has been said that Lake Travis and the surrounding areas is "God's Country," home to picturesque natural landscapes, abundant wildlife and a sunset to write home about. To protect the pristine Texas Hill Country, nature parks including Canyon of the Eagles, Hamilton Pool, West Cave Preserve and Wild Basin Wilderness Preserve, provide nature education programs and guided tours to help visitors fully appreciate native plants, animals and birds in their element.

LIFESTYLE

Celebrate
Austin's Active Side

Often coined "A City Within a Park," Austin is home to two-dozen greenbelts and over 200 parks, 12 of which include off-leash areas where Rover can roam free.

BY LIBBY DEAN HOPE

It's not hard to be active in a city like Austin. With more than 16,000 acres of green space, a chain of lakes along the Colorado River and more than 300 days of sunshine each year, opportunities for recreation and fitness abound. Whether you're into running, biking, or a friendly game of Frisbee, it's easy to get up and get moving in the fittest city in Texas.

Often coined "A City Within a Park," Austin is home to two-dozen greenbelts and over 200 parks, 12 of which include off-leash areas where Rover can roam free. Winding in and out of the city's parks are 50 miles of trails suitable for both recreational or expert hiking and biking. Seven-time Tour de France winner and Austin native Lance Armstrong helped put the city's biking community on the map, but long-time residents have been hitting the trails for decades. From two wheels to two legs, the trails also boost Austin's reputation as a runner's paradise. The most popular of all trails, the Town Lake hike and bike trail along the shore of the Colorado River, is busy sunup to sundown 365 days a year. The city's scenic beauty coupled with a supportive cast of running groups and businesses keeps Austin runners on their feet.

There are also plenty of other ways for fitness aficionados to get their feet wet...literally. Beginning in downtown Austin and stretching for some 150 miles west and north into the Texas Hill Country is the Highland Lakes system. Seven dams along the Colorado River helped create the six lakes, Lake Travis and Lake Austin within minutes of the city center. Water enthusiasts can go boating, waterskiing, canoeing, or rowing, many of those activities offered year-round.

Though known for its range of traditional sports, Austin's "weird" culture also cultivates some lesser-known activities like bouldering, frisbee golf, and windsurfing. Dodgeball isn't simply for middle school gym class anymore; it's popping up in sporting leagues across the city.

With endless opportunities to watch or participate in sports in and around Austin, the city remains a hotspot for people wanting to take advantage of the outdoors.

Top 5 Ways to Stay Cool in the Texas Sun

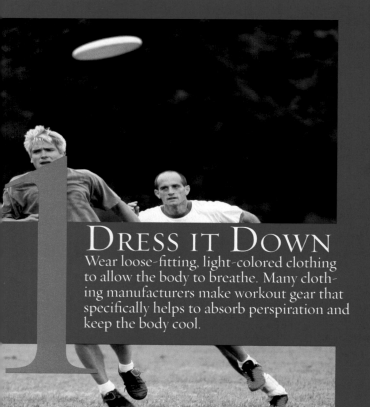

1

DRESS IT DOWN
Wear loose-fitting, light-colored clothing to allow the body to breathe. Many clothing manufacturers make workout gear that specifically helps to absorb perspiration and keep the body cool.

2

DRINK UP!
Drink lots of water before, during, and after exercising. Also, avoid caffeine or alcohol to prevent that unwanted, dry-mouth dehydrated feeling.

3

BE WHAT YOU EAT
Digestion actually generates body heat, so avoid hard-to-digest foods such as proteins. Instead, opt for lighter fare like fruits and vegetables that won't warm you up before your warm-up.

4

COOL DOWN
It's true. We lose a lot of heat through our head, but we also gain special vitamins when exercising in the sun. Wear a loose hat and pour water over your head periodically during exercise to cool the body and avoid sunburn during extensive sun exposure.

5

PLAN, PLAN, PLAN
Avoid exercising outdoors between 10am and 7pm on hot days and plan a shady route along a covered trail to dodge pavement that retains heat.

SPORTS & OUTDOORS

ALEX PHOTOGRAPHY

Impressive Equestrian Center...
...Incredible Equestrian Community

Since 1925 the Austin Polo Club has hosted the oldest team sport in history with expertise, flair, and fun. From competitive matches and tournaments to the riding disciplines of dressage, hunter/jumper, and cross-country as well as attentive staff for boarding facilities, the Austin Polo Club has served the demands and passions of the avid equestrian including:

- ♘ Three polo fields
- ♘ Outdoor and indoor arena facilities
- ♘ Hundreds of acres for trail riding
- ♘ Site use for private parties or corporate events

In the fall of 2008, the Austin Polo Club will move its world-class facilities to **THE VINEYARD** AT FLORENCE

Unlike any other master-planned community in the area, it will offer equestrian-friendly home sites along with a wealth of amenities including a winery, distinguished collection of homes, and an equine-centered lifestyle. Break into a canter now online at: www.thevineyardatflorence.com

AUSTIN
POLO
CLUB

512-626-1243   www.austinpoloclub.net

WHY DOES CARMELO ANTHONY
WEAR THE BRACELET?

He wears it to raise desperately needed funds for HIV/AIDS care services, education and vaccine development. Over half a million people have chosen to wear The Bracelet. What about you? Available at: Virgin Megastore, Ben Bridge Jewelers and other fine retailers. Or to order call 1-800-88-UNTIL or visit us at WWW.UNTIL.ORG.

UNTIL
THERE'S A CURE

Austin's Backyard

BY LIBBY DEAN HOPE

For many people, the ideal Saturday afternoon get-together with friends and family is a poolside backyard barbecue complete with a friendly game of football or horseshoes. The problem is not everyone has a grill, a pool or a backyard—and not everyone is always at home. But in Austin, you don't need your own house with a hefty mortgage to host your own al fresco affair. Shadowed by downtown's financial district and towering buildings is Austin's very own backyard.

Where the city's center meets the Colorado River is the heart of Austin's outdoor activities. Lady Bird Lake and its surrounding parks, trails and recreational areas have everything an apartment building doesn't. Spanning roughly five miles along the river bounded by two dams, Town Lake offers Austin residents and visitors a unique space for exercising, entertaining, or enjoying the great outdoors. Easily the busiest trail in the city, the Town Lake Hike and Bike Trail runs in a circular path around the river. Full of activity 365 days a year, the 10.1-mile trail is lined with shady oak trees and composed mostly of dirt and light gravel, a welcomed relief for long-distance runners from unforgiving concrete. For those who measure workouts in 15-minute intervals instead of 15-mile stints, the trail has six pedestrian bridges or walkways crossing the river, making it easy to plan a run, jog, walk or bike ride at varying distances.

For more hands-on sports, there are numerous ball fields

for baseball, football, soccer, and other activities at both Auditorium Shores and Butler Shores on the south side of Town Lake. Be forewarned, though. It's not uncommon for a Labrador to interrupt your game at Auditorium Shores. As one of the city's off-leash dog parks, man's best friend rules the grounds on sunny afternoons. A few rowing docks are tucked away just off the trail along the river where novice rowers or experienced scullers take to the water daily.

A stone's throw away from the shores of Town Lake is the 351-acre Zilker Metropolitan Park. Zilker has its own ball fields in addition to full-service picnic areas perfect for grilling hamburgers and bratwursts on the weekends. Be sure to check the calendar before packing the cooler and heading shore side. Both Zilker Park and Auditorium Shores host large outdoor concerts and events year-round, including the Austin City Limits Music Festival in late summer.

In the summer of 2007, the Town Lake area welcomed yet another enticing element to draw visitors to downtown's backyard: Town Lake Park. Located between Barton Springs Road and Riverside Drive just south of Auditorium Shores, the 21-acre, $7.3 million park will become what developers hope to be Austin's Central Park, echoing those in larger cities like New York. Also within the city's new centerpiece are the Palmer Events Center and the Long Center for the Performing Arts, giving Austinites even more reason to visit the latest attraction. With amenities such as a children's art garden, an oval-shaped meadow, and a concrete plaza with capricious fountain jets, the park is sure to appeal to children and adults alike.

The Town Lake area reminds people that despite the city's development, Austin is still committed to giving residents and visitors a place to be outside and respect the natural environment that is the foundation of the capital city. We're not all lucky enough to have a backyard, but we are lucky to be in Austin.

SPORTS & OUTDOORS

CELEBRATE GOLF

GREY ROCK GOLF CLUB

Just 15 minutes southwest of downtown, this club knows what it takes to make guests feel welcome. Guest will enjoy the challenges of their 18-hole Jay Morrish-designed course in championship condition, expert staff and superior dining in a unique Hill Country setting. Grey Rock Golf Club, 7401 Highway 45, 512-288.4297; www.greyrockgolfclub.com

FALCONHEAD GOLF CLUB

Designed by Chris Gray, Director of Design for the PGA TOUR, Falconhead Golf Club is America's first PGA TOUR Signature Series Course. Located in the beautiful Texas Hill Country, the course is maintained to exacting standards and the staff is friendly and helpful. Come and see why many people considered Falconhead to be the finest public golf experience in Austin. Falconhead Golf Club; 15201 Falconhead Blvd.; 512-402-1558; www.falconheadaustin.com.

THE GOLF CLUB AT STAR RANCH

Home of the "All You Can" special. Beautiful course with rustic ranch theme offers superb golf, restaurant, meeting, and tournament facilities. Also gives green fees, cart fees, range balls, breakfast, lunch and replays for one great price. Rated "Best Tournament Venue" by Avid Golf Magazine. The Club at Star Ranch; 2500 FM 685, Hutto, TX; 512-252-GOLF; www.starranchgolf.com

THE GOLF CONNECTION; 817-594-1016

The Golf Connection USA has added a second golf show to its annual line-up of 2008 Texas golf expositions with the purchase of the Austin Golf Expo. The Austin Golf Expo will be held at the Crockett Center in Austin on February 23 and 24th, 2008. The show kicks-off the 2008 golf year and is followed by Texas' largest golf show, the North Texas Golf Expo held March 7-9, 2008 at Dallas Market Hall. The Austin Golf Expo is a great opportunity to build brand recognition and customer loyalty through a broad television, radio and print advertising campaign. In serving the needs of our golf community, a portion of the golf show proceeds will be divided among several local Hill Country charitable organizations.

Celebrate
Indulging in Austin's Artistic Side

Whether looking back or stepping forward, the Austin art scene consistently upholds its reflection of Austin's diversity, creativity, and even its eccentricity.

BY KATHRYN CLELAND

Georgia O'Keefe once said,"To create one's own world in any of the arts takes courage." By her standards, the city of Austin would be a lion's den. Whether looking back or stepping forward, the Austin art scene consistently upholds its reflection of Austin's diversity, creativity, and even its eccentricity. The newly renovated Blanton Museum of Art on the University of Texas campus brings world-renowned artists and collections to Austin, as do the many downtown museums and galleries throughout the city. Together they are expanding upon and diversifying the already innovative, nationally- and internationally-recognized artistic culture in Austin. Art in Austin surpasses the walls of galleries and museums -- it reflects and builds upon countless aspects of the city's identity through varying media.

From folk art and quirky architecture to sculpture gardens and wall murals, Austin art takes on a ubiquitous nature in such a way that it can both catch you by surprise and be unknowingly overlooked. Building walls, easels for muralists, reflect the cultural diversity of Austin. One can find murals and historic renovations throughout the city, often by unexpectedly stumbling upon them. For those consciously searching art, the galleries and museums of the Downtown, University, and South Congress areas also offer variety and originality. Some venues combine literary readings with visual art, music, dance, theater, or film, proving that when it comes to art in Austin the possibilities are endless, the frontier infinite, and the style timeless.

In Austin, theatrical or dance performances take place nearly every night of the week. Like the wall murals, theaters in Austin can sneak up on the unexpected visitor, or even on some of the locals. A downtown coffee shop lives up to its name when one discovers its second identity as a hideout comedy theater and a neighborhood street quietly tucks away a playhouse. For the classical art lover, both the Austin Symphony Orchestra and that of the University of Texas offer an array of performances throughout the year.

While Austin is the reputed live music capital, its prestige spills over into other artistic realms. Local theatrical performances, museums, playwrights, and artists consistently gain national recognition while outside artists choose to perform in Austin for its reputation as an up and coming cultural capital. The influences and trends that inspire Austin's art scene diversify its artistic attributes, thus lending to the city's vast array of artistic resources. Locals immerse themselves in Austin's art on a daily basis while visitors flock here for a chance to dabble in it, if only for a weekend. So, whether it simply enhances your visit or colorfully inspires it, art in Austin will enlighten everyone from the average visitor to the most cynical critic.

Top 5 Reasons to explore Austin's Art Scene

1 The Impact
Many art exhibits in Austin send strong social messages, appealing to the eyes and the mind.

2 Its Ever-Present
Wherever you are in Austin, you're bound to stumble across a public art display: from wall mural to bejeweled, ten-foot guitars.

3 Its Ever-Changing
New museums, galleries, and programs spring up throughout the year in Austin, keeping art lovers of every kind interested and intrigued.

4 Its Interactive
Many art venues offer their own ways for locals and visitors to get involved in the art itself.

5 It Sets Austin Apart
We're keeping it weird, as always, and it is evident that the art here is like no other— as unique as the city itself.

ARTS

Founded in 2003, Randy Smith, Ltd. creates a unique perspective on Austin and The State of Texas. Through their photography they are able to share with people their love for this great state and the breath taking natural wonders and awe inspiring architectural marvels within it. Their work takes people where they haven't been before. They look for unique angles or the possibility of a montage whenever they visit a place and their real satisfaction comes from people enjoying their work.

Randy and Jackie Smith are actively involved in charities such as Make-A-Wish, The Lance Armstrong Foundation and The American Cancer Society. They are honored that their artwork can afford them to help improve their community. Also known for developing new products for Texas universities and colleges Randy Smith Limited develops unique pictorial perspectives that encompass each campus and what each school represents.

Find Randy Smith, Ltd., at local art festivals, arts & craft shows and at signings for various retailers. Please visit the Randy Smith Limited web site for more amazing imagery.

www.randysmithlimited.com
512-451-6815

On-line and at these other fine locations.
DECK•WALLS · UNIVERSITY CO-OP · THE STORY OF TEXAS · Wordisms HIGH QUALITY ART DIPLOMA, AND CERTIFICATE FRAMES PFLUGERVILLE, TEXAS

Check our website for locals events and other locations

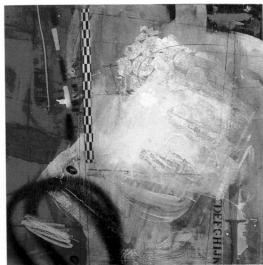

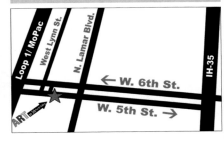

Art! At a Glance

	Architectural Elements	Ceramics/ Pottery	Collage	Drawings	Furnishings	Glass	Jewelry	Metalworking	Mosaic	Paintings	Photography	Portraiture	Printmaking	Sculpture	Textile/ Weaving	19th Century Artists
Art on 5th 1501 W 5th Street, 512-481-1111 www.arton5th.com				●						●				●		
Artworks 1214 West 6th Street #105, 512-472-1550 www.artworksaustin.com	●					●	●	●		●				●		●
Kathy Womack 411 Brazos @ 5th 512-288-0238 kwomack.com	●				●	●		●		●		●	●	●		
Randy Smith 512-451-6815 www.randysmithlimited.com											●					

ARTS

Find it in the West End

Most visitors to Austin quickly become familiar with the sights, smells, and sounds of its thriving downtown area. Bars hum with the laughing chatter of college students and urban professionals, dance clubs pump pulsing bass lines into the city's infamously balmy evening air, and you're just as likely to spot a delicious taco stand as you are to be offered a slice of New York style pie. While the famous bar scene gets most of the attention, Austin's downtown isn't just about grabbing a few drinks with friends — it is also home to one of the most vibrant art communities in Texas.

The Austin Museum of Art and the University of Texas' newly built Blanton Museum offer huge collections, but it's the small, independent galleries that truly create the local flavor of the city's art scene. Each gallery plays to its own niche in the art world, and until 2004 they were largely unallied. However, in September of that year, the owners came together to create the West End Gallery Night, named after the portion of downtown occupied by the galleries.

Just which part of downtown qualifies as the West End proper can be nebulous, but it's usually agreed to consist of the area around west 5th and 6th streets, extending eastward to Lamar Boulevard. Most patrons find it easiest to visit Art on 5th first, as it is more remote from the other galleries and offers better prospects for evening parking. From there, you may go one street over to 6th and hop to the remaining galleries. Though the art is the main attraction during Gallery Night, that doesn't stop anyone from enjoying the many coffee houses, bistros,

and bars in the immediate area as well.

Inthegalleriesaustin.com is the unsurpassed website available to showcase the Austin art scene. Visit this web site for a list of local gallery openings, a monthly calendar of events, celebrations, announcements and an easy to use map and directory page.

Urban Roots, Art on 5th, Lotus, Wally Workman, f8 Fine Art, Stephen L. Clark, Artworks, and Haven all participate in the event, held on the first Thursday of each month. Wine, cocktails and hors d'oeuvres are commonly served, and all the galleries stay open late, until 8:00 PM, to accommodate art browsers who work during the day. Many of the galleries plan the openings of new exhibitions to coincide with the night, and special events are also common.

The art exhibited runs the style gambit from impressionist to avant garde, and are in a variety of mediums. Local artists are featured most prominently, but some galleries have incredibly diverse collections — you are just as likely to see a 3D avant garde model as a Picasso print. f8 specializes in photography, Lotus in Asian art, and Art on 5th is known to have a broad collection.

If you're already acquainted with 6th street's lively bar scene, come out a little early on a first Thursday and experience the incredible art you've been missing. If you're unacquainted with the area as whole, you'll be in for the treat of Austin's nightlife and art scene at its most vibrant in one night. Spend your next first Thursday with the arts!

ARTS

Celebrate
Relax and Be Zen - It's Austin!

One of the best ways to give your body and soul some well-deserved attention is to head to one of the various day spas.

BY STEPHANIE MATLOCK

It's not hard to be active in a city like Austin. With more than 16,000 acres of green space, a chain of lakes along the Colorado River and more than 300 days of sunshine each year, opportunities for recreation and fitness abound. Whether you're into running, biking, or a friendly game of Frisbee, it's easy to get up and get moving in the fittest city in Texas.

Often coined "A City Within a Park," Austin is home to two-dozen greenbelts and over 200 parks, 12 of which include off-leash areas where Rover can roam free. Winding in and out of the city's parks are 50 miles of trails suitable for both recreational or expert hiking and biking. Seven-time Tour de France winner and Austin native Lance Armstrong helped put the city's biking community on the map, but long-time residents have been hitting the trails for decades.

From two wheels to two legs, the trails also boost Austin's reputation as a runner's paradise. The most popular of all trails, the Town Lake hike and bike trail along the shore of the Colorado River, is busy sunup to sundown 365 days a year. The city's scenic beauty coupled with a supportive cast of running groups and businesses keeps Austin runners on their feet.

There are also plenty of other ways for fitness aficionados to get their feet wet...literally. Beginning in downtown Austin and stretching for some 150 miles west and north into the Texas Hill Country is the Highland Lakes system. Seven dams along the Colorado River helped create the six lakes, Lake Travis and Lake Austin within minutes of the city center. Water enthusiasts can go boating, waterskiing, canoeing, or rowing, many of those activities offered year-round.

Though known for its range of traditional sports, Austin's "weird" culture also cultivates some lesser-known activities like bouldering, frisbee golf, and windsurfing. Dodgeball isn't simply for middle school gym class anymore; it's popping up in sporting leagues across the city.

With endless opportunities to watch or participate in sports in and around Austin, the city remains a hotspot for people wanting to take advantage of the outdoors.

Top Five Reasons Austin is the Best Place to Relax

1 Top Notch Spas

It is easy to relax in the Hill Country. Pamper yourself at some of the best locations to indulge your senses in the Lone Star state. Plus, our welcoming southern hospitality is just one of the benefits you can experience during your spa stay in Texas.

2 Nature Escapes

Check out parks, the greenbelt and hike and bike trails. Take a healthy break and enjoy swimming in year-round 68-degree waters of Barton Springs, or try visting Sculpture Falls.

3 Alternative Relaxation

Austin has many alternative methods to help you unwind such as meditation, yoga, Pilates or Tai Chi. Look to these invigorating activities for different ways to clear your mind and cleanse your spirit.

4 Getting Around is Easy

Find a diverse array of nature, culture, entertainment and pampering in Austin – all located in close proximity of one another. Ditch your car and unwind at theaters, parks and eateries within walking distance of your hotel.

5 Indulge in Outdoor Shopping

Take a break from the mall and look to SoCo and shops in the 2nd street district for some retail therapy. Getting out of that stuffy, crowded shopping center will literally be a breath of fresh air.

LEISURE

	Appointment Required	Hair Services	Manicures/ Pedicures	Waxing	Tanning/ Sunless Tanning	Make-up Application	Body Wraps/ Scrubs	Microdermabrasion	Facials	Acupuncture	Japanese Hair Straightening	Eyebrow/ Eyelash Tinting	Aromatherapy	Massage	Reflexology	Yoga	Permanent Make-up	Shopping/ Gifts
...CIENT WAY DAY SPA ...1 Koenig Lane, 512-502-0185 ...w.ancientwaydayspa.com				•	•		•	•	•			•	•	•				•
...Y FACE DAY SPA ...36 Research Blvd., #C206, 512-335-7770 ...w.babyfacedayspa.com		•	•	•		•	•		•			•					•	•
...ON CREEK SALON & SPA ...16 Crown Colony Dr, #101 512-280-2256 ...w.ocsalonanddayspa.com	•	•	•	•			•	•	•			•		•			•	•
...D GOLD BOUTIQUE & SPA ...1 East 5th Street, 512-473-2730 ...pointments, 512-350-6412				•				•	•				•	•				
...RACES SPA ...1 Balcones Drive, 512-453-7000 ...w.3gracesspa.com			•	•			•	•	•	•	•	•	•	•		•		•

Spa Etiquette

...HILE YOU SHOULD BE AWARE OF WHAT TO LOOK FOR ...HEN SEEKING SPA TREATMENTS, IT IS ALSO IMPORTANT ...NOTICE THAT CERTAIN ETIQUETTE CAN ALSO MAKE ...UR EXPERIENCE MORE ENJOYABLE. BE SURE TO FOLLOW ...ESE HELPFUL TIPS TO MAKE THE MOST OF YOUR PAMPER ...SSION.

• Knowing how much, when and to whom you ...ould tip is probably the most stressful part of your ...a visit. If you are satisfied with your treatment, it is ...mmon to tip between 15 and 20 percent. Be sure to ...k whether gratuity is included, since some spas will ...tomatically add it to your bill. You can include the tip ...en you pay, and the spa will handle the distribution if ...u had more than one treatment done.

• Always make sure to arrive at least 15 minutes early ...any treatment, so you have time to unwind and relax ...fore you get started. Most businesses cannot afford to ...sh their day back, so if you arrive late it will cut into your ...ssion. Arriving earlier will allow plenty of time to change ...o your robe and secure your belongings. You may even ...e yourself some time to enjoy a refreshing shower so that ...ur body can better absorb the treatments, take a quick ...p in the pool or try out the sauna if your spa has one.

• It is okay to be quiet. In order to help their clients ...l more comfortable, some therapists will choose to make ...nversation. However, it is perfectly acceptable to politely ...him or her know that you'd prefer not to chat. It is also

important to let your massage therapist know if you would like more or less force or if you are uncomfortable with the temperature in the room.

4. Undressing completely can be slightly unnerving, so only undress as far as you feel comfortable for your treatment. Most spas will offer paper underwear to wear during body treatments, or you may choose to bring a bathing suit to wear instead.

5. Leave anything that might interfere with your visit behind including jewelry, cell phones and other electronic devices. Consider leaving valuables at home, but also make sure to leave your communication devices in your locker. After all, the point of spa trip is to get away and relax. yourself escape.

Community Spotlight
Pamela Brewer

BY STEPHANIE MATLOCK

there, Brewer's relationship with the practice grew and she has been involved with it ever since. She has been teaching for about a decade and said she feels it was a necessary step for her. "When you teach something, it takes you to a different level of learning," she said.

Brewer previously taught at a gym, but was eager to try something different. She became involved with Ruta Maya through some of the employees who had taken yoga classes with her. "I wanted to do my own thing and see what happened," she said.

Through this connection, Brewer began teaching at the shop's new location about four years ago. The classes basically caught on through word of mouth and now there are free yoga classes six days a week. Saturday has become the busie day for yoga at the coffee shop, but customers are enthusiastic about yoga all week long – Rut Maya even introduced Happy Hour Yoga, a post-work class designed to help relieve stress.

If you're looking for a great place to relax and practice yoga, look no further than one of the best coffee shops in town, Ruta Maya. The combination may seem atypical, but it's time to leave those conventional thoughts behind – after all, this is Austin!

Most days of the week you will find Pamela Brewer at Ruta Maya doing what she does best – yoga. The local coffee shop has been ranked among the top 10 best coffee bars in the country and attracts customers from various parts of town and all walks of life. Brewer loves teaching yoga here due to the diversity of the people the shop attracts. From artists to realtors, Brewer said the classes allow people to get to know each other and find out what is going on around town. She is inspired by those she meets and said she feels the classes are beneficial to those who want to practice yoga but perhaps are not able to afford a pass at a gym or attend a yoga center. Best of all, the classes are free with a purchase at the bar.

Brewer became interested in yoga as a teenager when PBS shows started promoting yoga and Eastern philosophies. She began learning and reading about yoga and other practices such as meditation. From

Brewer's style focuses on Ashtanga yoga and she even spent time in India practicing her craft. She also teaches a more intense Vinyasa style at Ruta Maya on Tuesdays and Thursdays. Regardless of your level, there are plenty of options to choose from when picking a yoga style. "I think there's a style of yoga for everyone," she sai Brewer also teaches yoga at The University of Texas as part of their wellness program, along with private classes as well.

On her own time, Brewer relaxes by walking around Town Lake – recently renamed Lady Bird Lake in honor of another Texan, Lady Bird Johnson. A Dallas native who has enjoyed living in Austin for the past 20 years, Brewer loves to take advantage of all the festivals and music events around the city. "There's something for everyone!" she said.

A Day Off

COURTESY OF SAMIA BRIESCH,
OWNER AND SPA SPECIALIST,
3 GRACES SPA

NEED A FEW GOOD REASONS TO GET YOURSELF INTO THE SPA? HOW ABOUT TEN GOOD REASONS? GIVE YOURSELF AND SOMEONE YOU LOVE THE PERFECT RETREAT, RIGHT HERE IN AUSTIN! WHETHER YOU ARE VACATIONING OR YOU'RE A LOCAL AUSTINITE, A RELAXING DAY, OR EVEN AN HOUR, AT 3 GRACES SPA WILL HELP CURE YOUR TENSION, YOUR STRESS AND LIFT THE BLUES. DON'T WAIT ANOTHER DAY TO GET MUCH DESERVED REST AND RELAXATION!

10. You can choose from nine different massages to relax and indulge.

9. Wash away a bad day, feeling refreshed and renewed with better nails and skin.

8. Escape heavy Austin traffic by taking a quick detour to take a moment for yourself.

7. Gift certificates are available for all services we offer and are perfect for any occasion.

6. Prepare yourself for holiday trips, spring break and tropical vacations. We offer permanent hair removal and will leave your skin glowing for your getaway.

5. Problem Skin? No problem for us! We have facial peels, organic facial products and dermatologists' number one product: Obagi!

4. We offer a personal touch. Our owner is available and often brings in Mediterranean treats that will make every mouth water.

3. Enjoy time away with friends and take advantage of group packages. Come to 3 Graces Spa and be treated to four different services, plus wine and cheese.

2. We keep your schedule in mind. Our spa is open seven days a week, so you may come in when it is best for you.

1. Reveal your Goddess within!

BEAUTY.   CHARM.   JOY.

3GRACES
SKINCARE & SPA

CALL 453-7000 FOR
YOUR HOLIDAY
GIFT CERTIFICATES
SCHEDULE ONLINE AT
WWW.3GRACESSPA.COM

SERVICES

- PERMANENT LASER HAIR REMOVAL SYSTEM
- MASSAGE THERAPY
- BODY TREATMENTS
- MICRODERMABRASION
- ACUPUNCTURE
- PERMANENT MAKEUP
- MANICURE & PEDICURE
- CHEMICAL PEELS
- RESTYLANE
- RADIESSE
- OBAGI
- WAXING
- BOTOX

512.453.7000 • WWW.3GRACESSPA.COM
6101 BALCONES DR., STE. 100
(OFF 2222) AUSTIN, TX 78731

Celebrate
Getting the Goods in Austin

Take the short elevator trip downstairs to take advantage of all that your concierge can offer.

BY CP

With a reputation for achieving the impossible, your hotel concierge is sure to enhance your stay in Austin and is your best tool for unlocking the secrets of the city. Take the short elevator trip downstairs to take advantage of all that your concierge can offer.

Naturally, he or she is able to address the standard requests like making dinner reservations, purchasing tickets to concerts and events, coordinating travel arrangements, and booking tours to the best places in Austin, but those just skim the surface.

With a slew of personal contacts with local merchants, restaurateurs and service providers, your concierge can meet your needs regardless of how unique your request may seem. In the mood for Italian and need a place that is pet friendly? Or looking for live music and vegetarian cuisine? Your concierge knows the best spot in town, and will book your table so that you may effortlessly enjoy your experience.

Whether visiting Austin for business or pleasure, a gift of fresh flowers or box of sweets is a lovely gesture that is sure to be loved by your local friends, family or colleagues. By involving your concierge, it's a breeze! He or she will suggest the perfect gift for the occasion, place the order and coordinate delivery, making it easy to show your hosts how much you appreciate their hospitality.

Nothing else can stand up to the personalized service and care that a concierge is more than happy to provide. Make the most of your time in Austin. Do all you can to take in the city, and leave the rest to a concierge!

Top 5 Ways to Make the Most of Your Sta

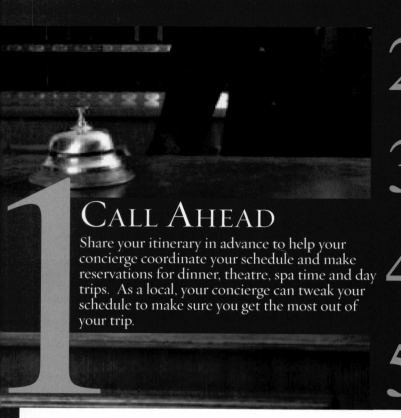

1 CALL AHEAD

Share your itinerary in advance to help your concierge coordinate your schedule and make reservations for dinner, theatre, spa time and day trips. As a local, your concierge can tweak your schedule to make sure you get the most out of your trip.

2 INTRODUCE YOURSELF

Make a point to get to know your concierge when you arrive. Building that relationship indirectly builds a relationship with countless influential people around town. Exchange business cards to ensure that you can easily get in touch when you need to.

3 FEEL FREE TO ASK

Whether you need materials prepared for a business meeting or travel arrangements for a last minute day trip, your concierges can make it happen, often at a be ter price that you could swing on your own. You'd be surprised what you can get if you ask!

4 BE REALISTIC

While concierges can sometime make the impos- sible possible, they cannot work miracles every time. Be patient and understanding when restaurants are booked or shows are sold out, knowing that your con- cierge did his best.

5 SAY THANK YOU

Although your concierge does not work for tips, showing your appreciation is always welcome.

CONCIERGE

THE *Art* OF GIVING FLOWERS

BY BETH O'REILLY
OF THE FLOWER STUDIO

Have you ever found it difficult to express your exact feelings and sentiments in a gift? One of the most popular ways to present a gift is to give flowers because they appeal to our senses and emotions, and they brighten up our lives. Coby Neal, AIFD and Beth O'Reilly, AIFD, of The Flower Studio, are aware of just how unique and special a hand-made and personally delivered piece of floral art is in today's age of pre-manufactured and mass marketed gift items.

Studies have proven that the presence of fresh botanicals in the work and home environment help people to maintain better mental health, according to Coby. He adds, "In the world of hectic living and the future looking towards the 'green environmental movement,' flowers offer the perfect opportunity to bring nature into our daily lives".

The silent messages of flowers speak loudly in conveying messages of love, regrets, celebrations, and every special moment that life has to offer.

Flowers are brought into the U.S. from places such as South America, Hawaii, New Zealand, Holland, Australia, Russia, and Egypt to name a few. According to Beth, flowers are more readily available than ever before, "It is amazing to think of all flower varieties available on the market today." Varieties such as the Green Goddess Calla Lily, King Protea, and Mokara Orchids are emerging onto the scene. Many of

these are considered couture flowers and are a far distance from carnations, sunflowers, and gladiolas. All flowers are beautiful, but exotic flowers are a new trend.

According to Coby, his customers rely on The Flowe Studio to create outstanding, innovative arrangements with exotic flora to make just right statement for any gift giving. "When a customer calls our shop wanting to send something special, our professional staff is capable of providing the perfect suggestion for the occasion with same day delivery service."

With many choices regarding the ordering of flower both Coby and Beth stress the importance of relying on your local, professionally established florist. To avoid scams such many online services, make sure there is credibility in the sho you entrust with your floral order.

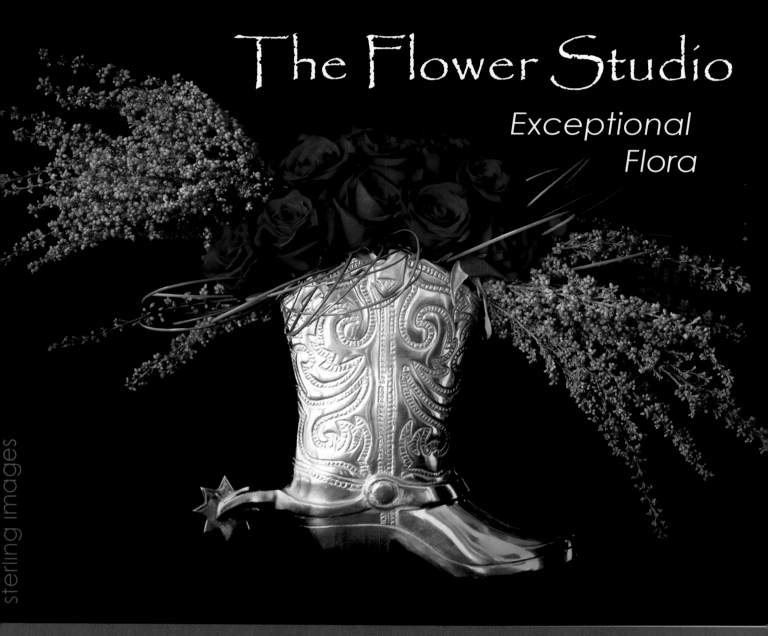

Traveler's Tipping Guide

BY CP

We all want show our appreciation for the services we receive when traveling, but it is difficult at times to stay abreast of the current etiquette. Here is a quick guide to thanking the folks who help you enjoy your trip.

Skycap
It is customary to tip $1 per bag, $2 for very heavy bags. An additional $1-$2 is optional for curbside check in.

Valet Parking Attendant
$1-3 is an appropriate tip to thank your attendant for parking or returning the car. It is not necessary to tip for parking, but always tip when your car is returned.

Hotel Doorman/Lobby Attendant
No tip is necessary for opening the door for you. If your Bellman hails a cap for you, thank him with $1. If he is especially helpful, offering dinner recommendations, directions, or other information, tip $5-$10.

Bellman/ Bell Captain
In most situations, $1-$3 per bag is suitable.

Housekeeping
$1-$3 per day is customary, depending on the amount of mess and the grade of the hotel. For higher-end hotels, you should leave $5-$10 per day. Leave the tip someplace obvious along with a note that clearly says "Housekeeping." Remember that chambermaids often rotate, so you need to tip daily.

Room Service
Gratuity is often included in the room service bill, so be sure to check. If not, 15%-20% of the bill is appropriate, depending on service.

Concierge
For ordinary advice and simple reservations, tipping is unnecessary. If he does something out of his way, like getting difficult restaurant reservations or tickets to a sold-out event, $5-$20 (or more) is the norm, depending on the difficulty. You can tip at the time of service or at the end of your stay.

Pool Attendant
No tip is necessary if you are only provided a towel. If your attendant gives you exceptional service by reserving lounge chairs, lending reading material, or giving you sunscreen, tip $3-$5.

Tour Guides
If you are pleased with the tour, you can tip $2-$5 to the tour guide for a full day tour. Tip a private guide more, 10%-15% for the entire party. Don't forget the driver! Giv $1-$2 to the driver, or more if he is helpful with luggage or souvenirs.

Taxi Service
Taxi drivers should receive 15% of the bill.

Limo Service
Tip your driver 15%-20% of the daily cost of service.

The Keeper of the Keys

BY JULIA ELIZONDO

"A mystery to many but a friend to all, the hotel concierge is a traveler's most overlooked ally." Austin is an innovative, unique community where anything goes and there is always something happening. There are always new sites to see, neighborhoods to explore, and hot spots to see and be seen. Where is the best place for brunch replete with celebrity sightings? Or, where can you find the best deal on antique textiles from India and Thailand? Your local concierge knows and is dedicated to providing the highest level of service. They educate themselves through daily encounters and experiences in their home city. It is their job to keep our finger on the pulse of what is happening in the city. There is plenty a concierge can do that even the savviest of travelers are not aware of- from getting tickets to a sold out event to scheduling after hours museum tours, even personal shopping.

Utilizing your hotel's concierge services can make for a more memorable trip, and save you time. It is their aim to improve your stay by giving you the time to focus on the things you need to do- or would prefer to do. Perhaps you would like to tour a few of the Hill Country vineyards or maybe catch an after hours jazz show downtown. Take the worry out of trying to find it yourself, have your concierge do it for you! If you are in town for business, make an impression on your clients by getting a little help booking a table at that impossible to get into restaurant. "I encourage guests to call as much as a month in advance before arriving to discuss the objectives of your trip, and be specific," suggests Jesse Knish, President, Austin Concierge Association. Are you here for an anniversary or a special someone's birthday? A concierge can plan your entire stay, from dinner reservations and events, to choosing the perfect gift and flowers. It is their job to make certain that you have an unforgettable experience while visiting, and to be sure that you remember them when planning your next visit.

Austin has it all and your concierge is only a phone call away to get it. Whether you are here for the art and music scene or you are looking for the perfect hiking trail or swimming hole, always ask your concierge to make the most of your stay. A concierge is there to achieve the impossible and to ensure that you enjoy Austin!

JESSE KNISH, PRESIDENT, AUSTIN CONCIERGE ASSOCIATION

CONCIERGE

Celebrate
Austin At Work

Austin's numerous historical sites and museums are iconic of the vibrant history and diversity in this region.

BY CARA HENIS

When you call the live music capitol of the world home, life becomes a blend of the arts, politics, educational achievement and technology. On any given day, Austinites curb boredom by enjoying some of the most stylish bars in the world, or experience the pleasures of the fine arts by viewing a ballet or an amateur improv troupes perform at the quirky coffee shops along Congress and Sixth Street. Austin's numerous historical sites and museums are iconic of the vibrant history and diversity in this region. As the fourth largest city in Texas and the 16th largest city in the United States, Austin is a hub for variety.

The majestic pink granite dome of the Capitol of Texas is a beautiful and historic part of the Central Texas skyline. Construction on the landmark was completed in 1888 and is second in size only to U.S. Capitol building in Washington D.C. As the political hub of Texas, Austin is at the center of state politics. Many activist groups and lobbyists head their campaigns in Austin. Every cause, whether concerned with the environment, education or business is represented in Austin. The city is known as a liberal oasis in a conservative state. While the areas within the city limits are usually heavily democratic, the outlying suburbs are usually more conservative. Austin remains highly visible in the national political scene as well with all eyes upon Texas' former governor George W. Bush serving as the current President of the United States.

You can't mention Austin to a Texan without some connection to college life whether you're thinking of the prestigious educational opportunities or the football.

According to CNNmoney.com, Austin is the fifth brainiest city in the country, with about 44% of residents over 25 having a bachelor's degree. This reputation has drawn a steady stream of employers and made Austin perfect for citizens who love lively political debates and literary discussions. Over 90,000 students in the area are enrolled in some sort of higher education. The University of Texas at Austin is by far the largest and most well known in the state. Ranked the 47th best university by U.S. News and World Report, The University of Texas at Austin is the academic flagship for the UT system. The UT Longhorns are at forefront of research and development throughout the world and are of course remembered for their 2006 championship football win. Students also come from around the state and country to attend smaller, private institutions such as Concordia, St. Edwards, and Huston-Tillotson and Austin Community College

Higher educational standards have attracted some of the most brilliant minds in business and innovative industries in the world. Dubbed 'the Silicon Hills,' Austin, especially in recent years, has noticeably become a center of commerce especially technology-based trade. In 2005 alone, roughly 2,000 patents were granted to Austinites. UT is third in the nation for annual number of patents earned. Venture capital investments in the area are also high. More than $12,000,000 was spent on biotechnology alone.

Thus, Austin is a metropolitan area for those who love to explore the arts, dapple in politics and investment, and experience big city living without sacrificing all perks.

Top 5 Reasons to Work in Austin

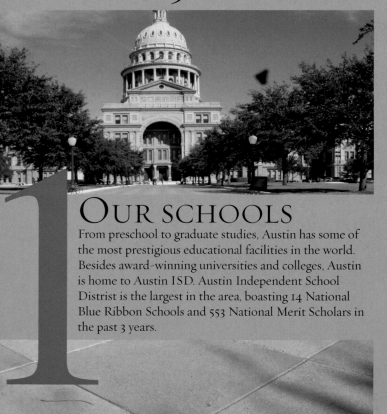

1 Our schools

From preschool to graduate studies, Austin has some of the most prestigious educational facilities in the world. Besides award-winning universities and colleges, Austin is home to Austin ISD. Austin Independent School District is the largest in the area, boasting 14 National Blue Ribbon Schools and 553 National Merit Scholars in the past 3 years.

2 Our jobs

No matter your areas of interest, Austin most likely has a bustling job market in that field. The number one employer in the area is The University of Texas, however, technology companies such as Dell Inc. and IBM are major players in the job market as well.

3 Our resources

Austin is chock full of places to improve your mind and your body. The city has numerous libraries, museums and fitness trails. The 17 University of Texas libraries, which are open to the public and have more than 8 million volumes available, are great places to go stretch the mind, while Town Lake's walking trails are perfect to work the body.

4 Our events

Whether you are interested in art, music, movies or shopping, Austin has plenty of each to try. Austinites have the chance to enjoy local bands at South by Southwest, a world-renowned music and film festival, or head down to South Congress Avenue for some of the best shopping in the city.

5 Our housing

Everything from luxurious townhouses to quirky urban-style lofts can be purchased with a little bit of exploration. The median average housing cost in the city is $173,700, which compared to the national average of $222,000, is quite a deal.

Next Stop: Silicon Hills

BY CP

Over the past two decades, the technology industry has provided an unprecedented opportunity for growth in Austin. Now proudly nicknamed "Silicon Hills," the Texas counterpart to California's "Silicon Valley," Austin is home to notable companies such as Dell, IBM, Freescale Semiconductor, AMD, Intel, Sun Micorosystems, Sematech, Apple and soon, the foremost industry giant: Google.

Talented techies from all over the nation are drawn to our beautiful city to be a part of a business sector that represents the largest number of employees than any number in Austin. Of course the highly acclaimed University of Texas, seated comfortably nearby, offers a constant source of young, fresh talent, allowing the industry to have sustained growth.

Generating a significant percentage of the income in Austin, the technology center has a huge impact on the local economy. Nurturing this sector is a priority for Austinites who recognize that the success of the technology industry plays a huge role in the future success and growth of the Texas Hill Country.

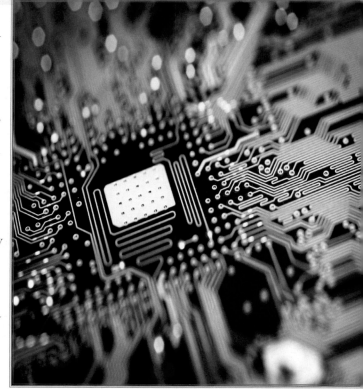

BUSINESS

Are you looking for the groundbreaking achievement, aggressive growth potential, and unlimited resources to excel? Couple that with a full continuum of strategic solutions, from early discovery to post-market support, and that's exactly what you'll find at **PPD**. As a leading global provider of contract and consulting discovery and development resources for pharmaceutical and biotechnology companies, we're in the business of making a difference. Our ability to help clients quickly bring new products to market enhances the lives of people all over the globe and instills a strong sense of pride and fulfillment in our team. It's the kind of breakthrough achievement you expect and deserve. Break new ground with PPD. The following positions are currently available with PPD Development, a subsidiary of PPD providing integrated drug development services.

break new ground

THESE POSITIONS ARE AVAILABLE IN OUR **AUSTIN, TX** LOCATION:

- **BIOSTATISTICS**
- **DATA MANAGEMENT**
- **CLINICAL OPERATIONS**
  - **CLINICAL PROJECT MANAGEMENT**
  - **CLINICAL RESEARCH ASSOCIATES**

Our location in **Austin, TX** merges excellent growth opportunities, the compensation and benefits of a global organization, and the unique quality of life only Austin can provide—exciting and academic opportunities of a university community, and the beauty of the Texas hill country.

To submit your resume online for these or other career opportunities, please visit us at www.ppdi.com.

A diverse workforce enables us to achieve breakthrough advancements — an Equal Opportunity Employer.

WWW.PPDI.COM

PPD®

Celebrate

A Night on the Town

> Austin is sure to promise anybody who loves the nightlife an eventful evening.

BY JAMES BRIDGES

When the sun sets and the city lights begin to glisten, another exciting night in Austin begins. Packed with great restaurants, bars, live music venues, theaters and an array of fine local beverages, Austin is sure to promise anybody who loves the nightlife an eventful evening. With all of the hustle and bustle of day-to-day life, Austinites and visitors alike deserve a break from their busy schedules to take advantage of this abundance of activity.

Austin's most happening areas, Sixth Street and the Warehouse District, can be found in the heart of downtown. This area, spanning from Second Street to Eighth Street, is lined with the city's trendiest bars and restaurants. Full of history and entertainment, this vicinity is always bursting with energy and movement, not to mention the sound of electric guitar riffs. With so much action on Friday and Saturday nights, Sixth Street is closed off to traffic to allow full access to nighttime visitors.

If you want to avoid the crowds of Sixth, but still want to experience Austin's bar scene, head over to Fourth Street and check out the fashionable warehouse district. As its name suggests, the distinctive bars and upscale restaurants in this area are all renovated warehouses from Austin's past. The history and ambience of this reborn, industrial zone will provide any visitor a unique experience. Though a bit pricier than the nearby Sixth Street, the warehouse district will amaze you with its trendy clubs and chic restaurants. You can enjoy a hot cup of coffee, indulge in an exquisite meal or simply relax with a few cocktails, all while soaking in Austin's rich history.

Maybe you're into finding an alternative to the bar scene. If so, take your party to one of the many theaters in the area. The only cinema in town where you can get a frosty mug of beer, enjoy a quality meal and catch a flick is the Alamo Drafthouse. This independently owned and operated cinema offers a mix of first-run, independent and classic films. For a stage show, visit either the State or Paramount Theaters on Congress Avenue that offer the best in classic and contemporary plays and musicals.

Live entertainment can be found around any corner of Austin. Whether it's catching a few laughs at a comedy club or enjoying some of the talented local musicians, the state capital is booming with it all. The city also hosts many exclusive festivals throughout the year. South by Southwest and the Austin City Limits Music Festival, for example, bring in a massive assembly of today's finest musicians and film makers from all over the world. These events, coupled with the everyday abundance of music shows, have made Austin the "Live Music Capital of the World".

When the moon comes out, Austin comes alive. Prepare yourself for a memorable night because this one-of-a-kind city has it all. The live music, wild clubs, friendly people and historical surroundings make Austin's nightlife experience truly unforgettable.

1 LIVE MUSIC

In 1991, Austin was given the prestigious title of "Live Music Capital of the World" when research found that the Lone Star capital had more live music venues per capita than any other city in the world. From reggae to rock and rap to Texas blues, Austin's nightlife is sure to offer enjoyable live music regardless of your taste!

2 BAR AND CLUB SCENE

Downtown Austin is famous for Sixth Street and the Warehouse District, a club and restaurant packed area that is full of excitement and entertainment. Stretching from Fourth to Sixth Street, you can find a melting pot of people, places, and activities.

3 THE GREAT OUTDOORS

Because of Austin's temperate weather and proximity to various rivers and lakes, party boats make for unique nightlife. These barges are excellent for large groups who want to party 'till the sun comes up. Austin is also home to North America's largest urban bat population, which can be seen from Congress Avenue Bridge at sunset.

4 THEATER

Catch a movie or play at one of Austin's many theaters. The Alamo Drafthouse offers an unique experience of dinner, drinks and cinema. If you would like to catch a performance, The State and Paramount Theaters produce the best in modern and classic plays

5 TEXAS BEVERAGES

Austin offers the best in Texas beers and wines. Enjoy a distinctive brew from one of Austin's 5 microbreweries or sip a glass of wine from one of central Texas' numerous vineyards. Regardless of your taste, there is something to please you.

AT A GLANCE — LOCAL ENTERTAINMENT

	Casino El Camino — 517 East 6th Street, 512-469-9330, www.casinoelcamino.net	Coyote Ugly — 501 East 6th Street, 512-236-8459, www.coyoteugly.com	J. Black's Feel Good Lounge — 710 W 6th, Suite B, 512-433-6954, www.jblacks.com	Maggie Mae's — 323 East 6th Street, 512-478-8541, www.maggiemaesaustin.com	Pete's Dueling Piano Bar — 421 East 6th Street, 512-472-PETE, www.petesdeulingpianobar.com	Rick's Cabaret — 8110 Springdale Road, 512-929-3939, www.rickscabaret.com	Saxon Pub — 1320 South Lamar, 512-448-2552, www.thesaxonpub.com	Yellow Rose — 6528 North Lamar, 512-458-2106, www.yellowroseaustin.com
Dining Available	●		●			●		●
Live Music	●			●	●		●	
Smoking Available	●	●	●	●			●	
Beer and Wine Only								
Full Bar	●		●	●	●	●	●	●
Patio or Outdoor Area	●		●	●				
Rooftop Seating				●				
Valet Parking						●		●
Family Friendly	●							
Sports Bars or TVs	●	●		●		●		●
Pet Friendly	●							●
Dress Code Enforced								
Weekend Drink Specials		●		●		●	●	●
Party Reservations Available	●			●	●	●	●	
Seating Reservations Available						●	●	
Weekend Cover Charge					●	●		
Credit Cards Accepted	●	●	●	●		●		●

Bringing you the best Austin has to offer.

Robert Hurst, nationally renowned for vibrant acrylic images portraying icons from the worlds of sports and music, has been the official artist for the Texas Sports Hall of Fame since 1997. His work is included in the collections of such notable athletes as Muhammad Ali, Reggie Jackson, Michael Johnson and Hakeem Olajuwon.

Located on Sixth Street in the heart of Austin's Historic Entertainment District, Maggie Mae's is an entertainment venue unlike anywhere in the world. Famous for live music that will have you rockin', a rooftop deck with a panoramic view of Austin's Skyline and a huge 26 foot screen, an English Pub and a gas-lit New Orleans-style courtyard, Maggie Mae's has been Austin's premier nightlife destination for over 28 years! Visit Us for an afternoon of cheering on your favorite teams, a night of dancing to live music or a few hours of relaxed fun...you're guaranteed a good time at Maggie Mae's!

- ONE BLOCK FROM CONVENTION CENTER
- MULTIPLE TELEVISIONS AND BIG SCREENS
- PRIVATE EVENTS FOR GROUPS UP TO 1,500
- PROFESSIONAL FULL SERVICE IN-HOUSE CATERING

SIXTH STREET
MAGGIE MAE'S
AUSTIN TEXAS

Icons

LIVE ROCK & ROLL
SPORTS BAR
ENGLISH PUB & GALLERY...

FEATURING ARTWORK
BY ROBERT HURST

ESTABLISHED 1978
323 E. SIXTH STREET - AUSTIN
TEL: 512.478.8541

MAGGIEMAESAUSTIN.COM

For Private Events Contact Marilyn at 512-989-1340

Background photo of Austin at Night by C. P. Origer

Banquet photos by getthepictureinc.com

Sixth Street Revealed

WHAT DO YOU KNOW ABOUT 6TH STREET BESIDES THE FACT THAT IT IS AN AMAZING PLACE TO SPEND YOUR FRIDAY NIGHT BAR-HOPPING, DANCING AND PEOPLE WATCHING? IT IS ONE OF THE BEST PLACES FO AT-YOUR-FINGERTIPS FOOD, COMEDY, ENTERTAIN-MENT, LIVE MUSIC, GREAT DRINK SPECIALS AND SOUTH-ERN CHARM. BUT, MORE THAN THAT, 6TH STREET IS PART OF THE HISTORY OF AUSTIN. AUSTINITES CELE-BRATE THAT LEGACY, AND HERE ARE A FEW THING YOU SHOULD KNOW BEFORE YOU VENTURE OUT TONIGHT:

1. Before it was 6th Street, it was Pecan Street, and it was the main business corridor running through the middle of downtown Austin 150 years ago. Imagine horse drawn carriages, cigar and feed shops and general stores (even a saloo or two!), and transport yourself to the modern midwest that was 1860s Austin. Our Spring an Fall Pecan Street Festivals honor the original name of this street.

2. Nothing marks the beginning of 6th Street better than the massive, beautiful Diskill Hotel that looms over Brazos and Sixth. Completed i 1886, it is a landmark held with pride that was once one of the largest hotels in the southwest. It's reportedly haunted, so don't miss the chanc to take a tour for yourself!

3. The seven blocks that mark 6th Street, from Congress to I-35, are comprised of countless hi toric buildings, each one with a unique history. Don't be afraid to ask your bartender for a story

4. On the weekends and during special events, 6th Street is pedestrian friendly and closed off from passing traffic. Halloween, Mardi Gras, ROT Rally, SXSW and every weekend after 11pm is a good time to strap on your shoes and explore downtown by foot!

ENTERTAINMENT

Saxon Pub Shares
a Few Austin Memories

COURTESY OF JOE ABLES, OWNER, SAXON PUB

1 JANUARY 2004
Magical night in Austin as many celebrities are in town for a benefit at the Music Hall. Several end up on stage at the Saxon as guests of Stephen Bruton: Bonnie Raitt, Eric Johnson, Michael McDonald, Mickey Rafael, Marcia Ball. No explanation necessary.

BONNIE RAITT AND MICHAEL MCDONALD

2 DECEMBER 2004
Joe Ely does a two night stand with Joel Guzman on accordion. Incredible show featuring this all time great singer/songwriter. Joe repeated this performance Thanksgiving weekend 2007.

3 DECEMBER 2006
Willie Nelson appears as a "special" guest for his daughter Paula's video shoot. Also appearing that day was Ray Benson, Carolyn Wonderland, Pauline Reese and George Devore. The best Sunday afternoon show ever!

WILLIE NELSON A
DAUGHTER PA

4 OCTOBER 1999
Kris Kristofferson sits in with the Resentments on a Sunday night. Picks up a guitar, attaches his harmonica and breaks into "Me and Bobby McGee". I actually had tears in my eyes as I was so proud to have this little venue. I still get chills thinking about that night.

5 Any night Los Lonely Boys were there. And they were there many nights as an opener for five dollar cover. The best show they ever did didn't happen at the Saxon, it happened as we were watching the Grammies when The Boys were announced as winners. I'll never forget my wife and I yelling so loud. We are extremely proud of these three brothers and having a small part in their climb to stardom.

THE
Saxon Pub
Austin's Home for Live Music

1320 South Lamar
(512) 448-2552
www.TheSaxonPub.com

Photo by Winker

ALL PHOTOS BY WINKE

★ How did I become ★

BREWMASTER?

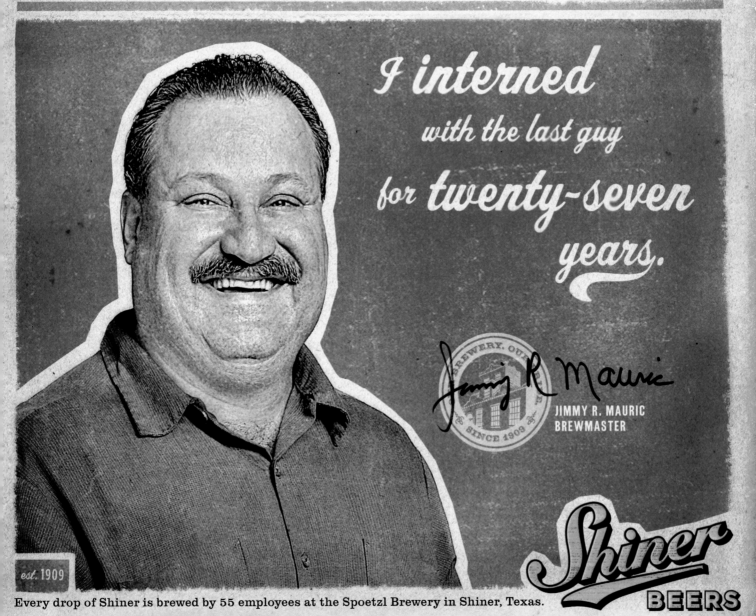

I interned
with the last guy
for **twenty-seven**
years.

Jimmy R. Mauric

JIMMY R. MAURIC
BREWMASTER

BREWERY, OUR
SINCE 1909

est. 1909

Shiner
BEERS

Every drop of Shiner is brewed by 55 employees at the Spoetzl Brewery in Shiner, Texas.

You can't possibly leave the Live Music Capital of the World without getting a taste of what our local music venues have to offer. But if the crowded downtown strip isn't your scene, don't worry! Just tune into ME, "Music and Entertainment" Television, a 24-hour network dedicated to showcasing and providing television exposure for regional artists as well as the hundreds of touring groups that make up the vibrant Texas live music scene.

Discovering and promoting new talent, as well as supporting established artists, is a top priority for ME. Its crews regularly visit Austin clubs including, Antones, Emo's, Stubb's, the Continental Club, Hill's Café and La Zona Rosa to film concerts in HD to spotlight musical acts in various genres. From Austin favorites like Bob Schneider, Joe, Ely and Del Castillo, to visiting artists like Collective Soul and the Black Crowes, you can find the bands that makes Austin's music scene great.

ME is Austin's entertainment resource, with venue schedules, artist information, interviews and local live music shows every night at 7pm on ME Live! ME represents different musical genres and areas of the arts community with numerous original programs highlighting everything from filmmakers to art galleries, and musicians to the ballet. In addition, ME's mostly music line-up spotlights live performance footage, concept music videos, as wells as biographies, reviews, restaurant tours and much more!

ENTERTAINMENT

Celebrate
The Special Taste of Austin

When tourists look beyond their expectations, they truly experience Austin, and in doing so, become more than a tourist.

BY CHRISTINE CHA-SARTORI

Although Austin has often been pigeonholed as a one-note wonder of Tex-Mex and barbeque, there's more to Austin cuisine than tacos and brisket. Beyond the clichéd culinary humdrums lies a tradition of oddball character and an innately ingrained quirkiness, which has manifested itself in the diverse array of Austin dining. Alternative restaurants serving vegan and vegetarian delights inundate the city with its quintessential hippie flair. Restaurants devoted to organic, free-range and hormone free products also add to the green earth vibe while promoting healthy living. The very definition of a restaurant has been questioned with trailers and stands popping up all around the city, producing some of the finest fare found in and around town.

Austin is renowned for its unique take on traditional Mexican food, but what of other nationalities? Austin's diverse cultures have taken root in this international city, yielding a multitude of ethnic restaurants and hybrid cuisines. Different districts are known for their ethnic specialties - Riverside brings authentic Mexican food, North Lamar fosters some of the best Korean in Austin, and further North on Lamar is home to a large Indian food community.

Sometimes, making your own meal is the best way to get a feel for a city. Swing by any of the numerous community markets to find local ingredients at the peak of their freshness. The shopping experience will put you in touch with the neighborhood and offer you a chance to experience the everyday life of an Austin citizen.

Austin is also known for fine dining. The movement of haute cuisine restaurants sweeping the city is easily accessible to all due to their casual elegance and low prices not found in other big cities like New York City and Los Angeles. Steakhouses and other meat driven fine dining establishments are especially popular; this is Texas after all. The impeccable quality of Texas beef and the talented chefs who prepare such delicacies should not be missed.

Widely recognized for their devotion to small businesses and the restaurant business is a prime industry for small business entrepreneurs. The personal touches and pride are palpable in every private or family owned business, particularly food establishments. Grabbing a bite to eat at a local joint satisfies your stomach while boosting community morale.

Our city offers a wide range of culinary possibilities. Every outing can be a little different, a little special, no matter what your budget happens to be. When tourists look beyond their expectations, they truly experience Austin, and in doing so, become more than a tourist. They become Austinites.

Top 5 local Beverages you Should Try

1 Mexican Martini
Austin's premier drink that is always bursting with alcohol. Keep in mind, most restaurants serve an entire shaker of the tequila concoction for every order so don't overdo it.

2 Local Beer
Several microbreweries are located within or just outside city limits. Order one at a bar or take a tour of the facilities. Most tours end with a beer tasting for all customers over 21, free of charge.

3 Margarita
Another tequila classic that has swept Austin. Austinite love the cool, refreshing bite of margaritas on our hot summer days. Add a basket of chips and salsa for a true taste of Austin.

4 Texas Wine
Texas wineries are making their mark on the wine worl The climate and fertile soil lend themselves to producir high-quality whites and reds. For an inside look, take a trip along the Texas wine trial located just outside of Austin to visit 21 distinguished wine producers.

5 Tea
There's a reason the nickname "Texas tea" belongs to a highly prized commodity. Texans love their tea, sweetened, alcoholic, iced or otherwise and many order with every meal.

DINING

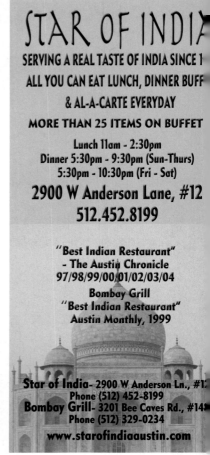

DINING

DINING

Market Fresh

BY CHRISTINE CHA-SARTORI

In recent years, Austin has transformed itself into Mecca for followers of green Earth alternative lifestyles. Scores of gourmet markets have sprung up around town, granting Austinites and visitors alike bounty of produce and specialty goods year round. Organic living is especially prevalent as evident by the exponential growth of market chains and the integration of hippi culture into everyday Austin life. In additio to the propagation of trendy mega marts, t boom of granola-bound, nature-loving folk has prompted numerous farmers' markets pop up in and around Austin.

Vendors in farmers' markets are required to grow or produce everything th sell. That means you are getting local prod from the farmers themselves. The proximity to the farmlands and lack of a middlem. translates to savings and quality for every market shopper. The downfall and beauty farmers' markets lies in the strict adherenc to seasonality. There are no apples flown in from Chile, nor organic avocados shipped from California; there are, however, strawberries grown in a patch just beyond interstate highway 35, tomatoes plucked from th vine the morning of your purchase and lam slaughtered mere miles away. Every fruit, vegetable and protein may not be available, but what is on hand will most certainly be cream of the crop.

Merchants are not simply marketin their goods – they are offering a way of life They will happily give you a tutorial on the best way to raise livestock or the finer poin of composting while you peruse the selection. It is interesting to get their take on th benefits of organic, free range and hormon free products. The farmers themselves are highly qualified, competent sources of valuable, straightforward information on some the perils of mass farming such as pesticide and overcrowding. Also, when stopping at stand, vendors will inevitably offer you a de cious array of samples, which also happens be the primary reason most patrons wake u before 10 a.m. on a Saturday. Loitering is h the fun of visiting a farmers' market.

Texas's rich soil and subtropical climate makes it an ideal spot for agricultur endeavors. Small farmers can generate a surfeit of organic products year round to th delight of Austin consumers. Take the oppo tunity to explore the markets and, in doing so, soak in a bit of Austin culture.

DINING

Ciao Down!

BY SHANNON SKINTO

Romantic, lush, bold, colorful, ageless; these are words that might come to mind when imagining the Italian landscape and fortunate for those in Austin, there is an array of Italian restaurants that are happy to meet these vivid expectations. Italians are prolific creators of some of the world's best art, music and literature. Their reputation for delectable food is without comparison and it is no wonder that penne and pesto has made its way to the American dinner table. One need not travel to Tuscany, however, to find a delightful selection of Italian cuisine options, when Central Texas boasts a substantial selection of authentic Italian restaurants. Explore your options within Texas and discover a piece of Tuscany in your own backyard.

Whether strolling down the fashionable Via Veneto or Austin's own Barton Springs, keeping in mind a few rules when you sit down at an Italian restaurant will make your experience not only more enjoyable, but perhaps more authentic.

A reputation for a laid-back lifestyle is more than deserved to the average Italian. Most Italian towns take siesta in the early afternoon after a midday meal to spend time with their families or to respite. It is not uncommon to see parks and town squares dotted with people reading books or enjoying the warmth of the Mediterranean sun. Italy is not a land known for strict rules but where every Italian might put his foot down is during mealtime. After a millennium perfecting the art of cuisine, Italians might have a thing or two to teach a Texan.

Most bona fide Italian breakfasts' consist of a cappuccino, and for those with a heartier appetite, perhaps a side of yogurt. Lunch and dinner are taken far more seriously and, traditionally, the meal is served in a series of small-portioned courses. The order of the courses is significant, with the fish or meat served foremost with a petite side of vegetables or a salad. A subsequent course would be a sample of cheese and a selection of fresh fruit. third course would often be a sweet dessert accompanied an espresso (conventional coffees made with milk or crea are held in reserve solely for breakfast). For those with a ta

A Pinch Amore!

When you're looking for more, better, different, you'll always find it at Carmelo's Ristorante. From more choices of authentic Italian cuisine to more selections of fine wines, from more private rooms for meetings, banquets and receptions to more live accordion music, from more elegant tableside cooking to more convenient valet parking, our belief is always amore the better!

Lunch Weekdays
~
Dinner Nightly

Wireless Internet Available

r pleasure, your repast would be polished
f with ammazzacaffe (Grappa or Amaro).

Bread is rarely eaten beside pasta.
abitually, bread is served on an empty
ble to greet guests. Butter is never served
ith bread but one will often find olive
l as an optional accompaniment with a
eshly baked loaf. Forget the heavy, creamy
lad dressings most Americans enjoy on
eir greens; in Italy, it is oil and vinegar
at flavors their leafy concoctions. Enjoy
chilled bottle of mineral water with your
eal. Soda and milk is considered a child's
rink; Italian adults prefer the bubbly
freshment found in a frosty Pellegrino. If
ubbly water isn't for your palette, ask for
glass of wine. Chilled white wine is lovely
ith fish and a warm red compliments most
eats.

Italian dining is more than just a
eal; it is sumptuous experience that will
ave you starry-eyed. Do as the Romans
o and revel in the warmth of the Italian
mbiance that Austin restaurants provide.

Carmelo and Luisa Mauro
t's all in the family!

Dining Menu

COURTESY OF MANUEL'S

	Average Entree Cost	Breakfast	Lunch	Dinner	Sunday Brunch	Water View	Patio Seating	Full Bar	Beer & Wine Only	Late Night Dining	Outdoor Smoking	Family Friendly	Credit Cards Accepted	Bus Parking	Valet Parking	Live Music	Reservations Available	Catering	Banquet Capacity
III Forks, 111 Lavaca St., 512-474-1776, 111forks.com	$$$			●				●			●	●	●		●	●	●	●	65
Austin Land & Cattle, 1205 N. Lamar Blvd., 512-472-1813, austinlandandcattlecompany.com	$$$		●					●			●	●	●				●		35
Banderas at the Renaissance, 9721 Arboretum Blvd., 512-795-6100, renaissanceaustin.com	$$$	●	●	●	●			●				●	●		●		●		
Benihana, 9070 Research Blvd #305, 512-451-7505, benihana.com	$$$		●	●				●				●	●				●		
Blu Parrot, 16107 FM 2769 Volente, TX, 512-258-5109, thebluparrot.com	$$		●	●		●	●	●		●	●	●	●			●	●	●	
Bombay Grill Indian Restaurant, 3249 Bee Caves Rd., 512-329-0234, bombaygrilltexas.com	$		●	●	●				●			●	●	●			●	●	30
Café Blue, 8714 Lime Creek Rd, 512-996-8188, cafebluetx.com	$$		●	●	●	●	●	●		●	●	●	●			●			
Cannoli Joe's, 4715 US Hwy 290 West, 512-892-4444, www.cannolijoes.com	$$		●	●	●			●			●	●	●						100
Cantina Laredo, 201 W. 3rd St., 512-542-9670, cantinalaredo.com	$$$		●	●	●		●	●			●	●	●		●	●	●	●	
Carlos N' Charlie's, 5973 Hiline Rd, 512-266-1683, cncaustin.com	$$		●	●		●	●			●	●	●	●	●				●	1500
Carmelos Ristorante, 504 E. 5th St., 512-477-7497, carmelosrestaurant.com	$$$		●	●			●	●			●	●	●	●	●	●	●	●	300
Cool River, 4001 Parmer Ln., 512-835-0010, coolrivercafe.com	$		●	●			●	●		●	●	●	●	●	●	●	●	●	●
County Line, 6500 Bee Caves Rd., 512-327-1959, 5204 FM 2222, 512-346-3664, countyline.com	$$		●	●	●						●	●				●		●	120
Docs Motorworks, 1123 S. Congress, 512-448-9181, 5207 Brodie Lane, Ste. 100, 512-892-5200, docsaustin.com	$		●	●			●	●		●	●	●	●	●	●			●	250

Per Entree in Dollars, $ = 1-10; $$ = 10-15, $$$ = 20+

DINING

Couples Night... Ladies Night... Romantic Celebration...

Whatever your occasion, The Melting Pot is the perfect night out.

Northwest Austin
13343 Research Blvd
(at Anderson Mill Rd.)

Downtown Austin
305 E. Third St.
(1/2 Block from Convention Center)

Call 512.401.2424
for Reservations.

The Melting Pot.®

a fondue restaurant

Dip into something different.®

www.meltingpot.com

fondue coast to coast | locally owned and operated

fine aged cheeses | assorted wines | seafood and steaks | chocolate fondue

DINING

	Average Entree Cost	Breakfast	Lunch	Dinner	Sunday Brunch	Water View	Patio Seating	Full Bar	Beer & Wine Only	Late Night Dining	Outdoor Smoking	Family Friendly	Credit Cards Accepted	Bus Parking	Valet Parking	Live Music	Reservations Available	Catering	Banquet Capacity
EASTSIDE CAFÉ 2113 MANOR ROAD 512-476-5858 EASTSIDECAFEAUSTIN.COM	$ $		●	●	●				●		●	●	●				●	●	32
EL GALLO 2910 S. CONGRESS 512-444-6696 ELGALLORESTAURANT.COM	$	●	●	●			●	●			●	●	●			●	●		75
ESTANCÍA CHURRASCARÍA 4894 HIGHWAY 290 W., SUNSET VALLEY 512-892-1225 ESTANCIACHURRASCARIA.COM	$ $		●	●				●				●	●	●			●		120
FOGO DE CHAO 309 E. 3RD ST. 512-472-0220 FOGODECHAO.COM	$ $ $		●	●				●			●	●	●	●	●		●		100
FRANK AND ANGIE'S 508 W. SIXTH ST 512-472-3534	$		●	●			●		●		●	●	●						
HUT'S HAMBURGERS 807 W. SIXTH STREET 512-472-0693	$		●	●					●			●	●						
IGUANA GRILL 2900 RR 620 512-266-8439 IGUANAGRILLAUSTIN.COM	$		●	●	●	●	●			●		●	●			●		●	
IRON CACTUS 10001 STONELAKE BLVD., 512-794-8778 606 TRINITY ST., 512-472-9240 IRONCACTUS.COM	$ $		●	●	●		●	●		●		●	●				●	●	800
JOE DIMAGGIO'S ITALIAN CHOPHOUSE 11410 CENTRY OAKS TERRACE 512-835-JOED WWW.JOEDIMAGGIOSRESTAURANT.COM	$ $ $		●	●			●	●		●		●	●	●	●		●		
KONA GRILL 11410 CENTURY OAKS TERRACE 512-835-5900 WWW.KONAGRILL.COM	$ $		●	●			●	●				●			●		●		40
MANUEL'S 10201 JOLLYVILLE RD., 512-345-1042 310 CONGRESS AVE., 512-372-7555 WWW.MANUELS.COM	$ $		●	●	●		●	●		●		●	●			●	●	●	●
MELTING POT 13343 HWY 183 N. SUITE 450 512-401-2424 MELTINGPOT.COM	$ $			●				●			●		●		●		●	●	44
MESA RANCH 8108 MESA DR. 512-853-9480 MESARANCHAUSTIN.COM	$ $		●	●			●					●				●	●	●	100
THE OASIS 6550 COMANCHE TRAIL 512-266-2441 OASIS-AUSTIN.COM	$ $		●	●	●	●	●					●	●			●	●	●	1200
RUTH'S CHRIS STEAK HOUSE 107 W. SIXTH ST. 512-477-7884 RUTHCHRIS.COM	$ $ $			●				●				●	●	●	●		●	●	100

Per Entree in Dollars, $ = 1-10; $$ = 10-15; $$$ = 20+

	Average Entree Cost	Breakfast	Lunch	Dinner	Sunday Brunch	Water View	Patio Seating	Full Bar	Beer & Wine Only	Late Night Dining	Outdoor Smoking	Family Friendly	Credit Cards Accepted	Bus Parking	Valet Parking	Live Music	Reservations Available	Catering	Banquet Capacity
STAR OF INDIA RESTAURANT 2900 W. ANDERSON #12 512-452-8199 STAROFINDIAAUSTIN.COM	$		●	●					●			●	●	●			●	●	
STARLITE 407 COLORADO ST. 512-374-9012 STARLITEAUSTIN.COM	$ $			●	●		●	●				●				●	●	●	
TREE HOUSE ITALIAN GRILL 2201 COLLEGE AVE 512-443-4200 TREEHOUSEGRILL.COM	$ $				●		●					●					●	●	
WATERLOO ICE HOUSE 8 LOCATIONS IN AUSTIN WATERLOOICEHOUSE.COM	$	●	●	●			●		●	●	●	●				●	●	●	●

Per Entree in Dollars, $ = 1-10; $$ = 10-15, $$$ = 20+

Austin's Brunch Scene SUNDAY MORNING IN STYL

SUNDAY IS THE BEST DAY OF THE WEEK TO RELAX. IT'S THE DAY OF REST AND WHAT BETTER WAY TO SPEND IT THAN WITH YOUR FAMILY AND FRIENDS AT A DELICIOUS BRUNCH. MANY OF THE RESTAURANTS IN AUSTIN THAT OFFER SUNDAY BRUNCH ALSO PROVIDE ENTERTAINMENT IN THE FORM OF LIVE MUSIC OR ROCKIN GOSPEL. LARGE BUFFET STYLE SPREADS ARE POPULAR AND THE MIMOSAS ARE SURE TO FLOW. WHETHER BRUNCH IS YOUR FAVORITE AFTER CHUCH ACTIVITY, OR YOUR WAY OF SPENDING A WARM TEXAS AFTERNOON WITH YOUR FRIENDS- YOU WILL FIND IT A VALUABLE EXPERIENCE!

CANTINA LAREDO- Serves Sunday brunch from 11am-3pm. Brunc entrees are served with a complimentary Mimosa or Bloody Mary. Enjoy the true taste of authentic Mexican cooking in the hip 2nd street district.

CAFÉ BLUE- Saturday and Sunday brunch served on the scenic shores of Lake Travis from 10am-2pm. Offering fine hill country cuisine. A relaxed and beautiful setting.

IRON CACTUS- Sunday brunch served at their downtown 6th str location and their uptown location on Stonelake from 10am-3pm $13.95 adults, $7.95 for kids 12 and under and $11.95 for seniors.

IGUANA GRILL- Serves brunch Saturday and Sunday from 11am-2pm over-looking beautiful Lake Travis. They feature migas, huevos, and chilaquiles. Kid's brunch menu included.

THREADGILL'S- Brunch is from 10-2 every Sunday. We feature various local gospel bands. There is no extra charge for th music. You can see a schedule on our website, www.threadgills.co Our brunch is buffet style. Adults are $10.95 children under 12 a $4.95. We feature migas, pancakes, omeletts, with favorite sides o sausage, bacon, grits, biscuits & gravy.

STARLITE- Serves Sunday brunch. Includes an extensive brunch menu with many sides to choose from. Impressive cocktail menu including Mimosas, Bloody Mary's and Bellinis.

Sip and Surf.
Or dine and unwind.

Decisions, decisions.

From the uber-cool cyber café, *@ustinbytes*, to the super-inspired cuisine of *Banderas–A Texas Bistrot,* the Renaissance Austin Hotel serves tech-savvy and Texas-splendid hospitality in style.

Whatever your decision, it's a smart one.

@ustinbytes – eat. drink. connect. Chat online at private computer stations or on your laptop while savoring Starbucks® coffee and snack. Chat in person with friends while sipping a fine wine. Either way, you'll click with our cyber café.

Banderas–A Texas Bistrot – Stellar lunch and dining selections rounded up from all across the Lone Star State in an upscale, yet relaxed setting. Saddle up and dig in!

Your special occasion will be even more special hosted in our impressive new event center debuting late spring 2008.

Uniquely Renaissance. Distinctly Austin.

RENAISSANCE®
AUSTIN HOTEL

9721 Arboretum Blvd. • Austin, Texas
512-343-2626 • 800-468-3571
renaissanceaustin.com

YANSI FUGEL®
Courtesy of The Garden Room
Travel Jersey™
ultimate packable knits

Celebrate
Chic Shopping in Austin

...you'll find that every district in Austin is filled with local shops and eateries. Handmade goods and services are essential to Austin's prosperity.

BY CHRISTINE PHAM

For some fashion gurus, Austin may not be the first place to come to mind when considering the fashion capitals of the world. But it's places like Austin where trends and fads are born because quite frankly, the last thing any Austinite wants is to look like everyone else. In embracing the coveted "weird," original lifestyle that is key to Austin, the idea is reflected on the ensembles of the people around this city. Austin is certainly at the top of the originality list.

Any local knows that relatively small cities with huge personalities rely on local business. That's why you'll find that every district in Austin is filled with local shops and eateries. Handmade goods and services are essential to Austin's prosperity. As this city is steadily growing in popularity and population, it is attracting attention from corporate America. Preferring not to be bombarded by machines of cheap labor, the people of Austin have developed organizations aimed towards tourists and Austinites alike to support local businesses. Steve Bercu, local business owner of BookPeople and founder of The Austin Independent Business Alliance (AIBA). With 350 members, all of whom are independent businesses, this alliance organizes annual events and local activities in hopes of attracting people to the funky-chic charm of local shops and boutiques.

All of these local shops and eateries are spread across the many shopping districts of Austin. Which, of course, means every two steps you take will lead you to something new. No two shops are the same, and there is so much to see because each boutique has something different to offer -- from leather handbags to embellished belt buckles and organic linens to retro lampshades. Whether you're looking for an interesting vintage piece, shopping at the local food market there, or finding an interesting gift for a friend, Austin has everything you need to make a statement.

While you're here, take advantage of more than just the live music. Be sure to visit South Congress, South Lamar, Guadalupe (known to locals as "the drag"), and uptown favorites, including The Domain and The Arboretum. Budget plenty to time to enjoy! You'll easily lose track to time searching in the glamorous shops owned by Austin residents or through earthy fabulous finds recycled into wearable works of art. Remember that you are not only working to look your best, but you are helping to support local

TOP 5 PLACES TO SHOP TIL YOU DROP

1 SoCo aka South Congress Ave

A pedestrian-friendly atmosphere giving New York City's SoHo a run for its money where Austinites and visitors alike can relish in the wide-ranging fashion from classic vintage to modern chic.

2 SoLa aka South Lamar Blvd

An area of offbeat shopping and dining, SoLa offers an array of local shops and restaurants along with a fantastic music scene for all shoppers strolling down this street.

3 Sixth Street

As Austin's best-known street, this strip is the core of Austin's live entertainment. It not only offers unique shops but the amazing live music echoes throughout Austin.

4 The Drag aka Guadalupe St

Located on the western edge of the University of Texas at Austin, the Drag is home to string of eclectic shops and eateries where you are sure to find the best in cool, funky garb and gifts.

5 Uptown at The Domain

A relatively new shopping district established in early 2007, this chic area is becoming Austin's premier shopping destination with its haute couture and home fashions.

SHOPPING

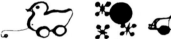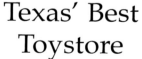

SHOPPING

Shopping At a Glance!

26 DOORS SHOPPING CENTER

Whether you're looking for fabulous food, gifts, original toys, or clothing, it can be found at 26 Doors, located in the heart of mid-town Austin. The shopping center is an Austin original. The central plaza—featuring a bronze sundial—is a perfect meeting place for friends, family and kids. Courtyards feature fountains and beautiful landscaping. Open seven days. 1206 W. 38th Street

ALLENS BOOTS

Founded in 1977, this store is really Allens boots, hats, pants, shirts, accessories, gifts and more! They've corralled two stores full of your kind of merchandise, from simply fine to pretty fancy. Remember: for Western wear, Allens is your one-stop shop. Open seven days. Allens Boots; South, 1522 S. Congress Ave.; 512-447-1413; Round Rock, 2541 S. IH-35; 512-310-7600; www. allensboots.com

AMELIA'S RETRO-VOGUE & RELICS

Has A New Home! 2213 So. 1st, amongst the other eclectic El Corazon shops! Still devoted to bringing you the best classic and old-school vintage for women, men and children; lamps, linens, eye wear, furniture, and decorative items with flair. Vintage styles also available. Call for hours, events schedule, directions: 512-442-4446, 2213 So. 1st, Austin, Tx, 78704

THE ARBORETUM

A unique shopping experience, the Arboretum gently beckons you to casually shop the beautiful and relaxed park-like setting that is home to more than 40 fine shops and restaurants in Austin's premier retail area. The Arboretum, open since 1985, is an Austins landmark. Visit the marble cows. Monday-Saturday 10 a.m. - 9 p.m. and Sunday 12:00 noon - 6:00 p.m. Some store and restaurant hours may vary. The Arboretum, 10000 Research Blvd.; 512-338-4437; www.simon.com

BARTON CREEK MALL

If you love shopping, you'll love shopping at Barton Creek Square with its more than 180 speciality retailers and anchor stores Dillard's, Macy's, JCPenney, Nordstrom and Sears. The center is located within 7 minutes of I-35 and downtown Austin, Texas and is accessible from Loop 1 and Highway 360. For a complete listing of our speciality retailers visit www. simon.com.

BEAD IT

Austin's Largest Bead Store! Four rooms filled to the brim with vintage glass, plastic, wood and other rare items. Also offering pendants, components, parts, findings and other treasures. Large selection of precious and semi-precious gemstones. Spacious, relaxing classroom where all are welcome to come and create. 2058 South Lamar; 512-693-2323; www. beaditaustin.com

CALLAHAN'S GENERAL STORE

It's like nothing you've ever seen before! Our feet are planted firmly i tradition with our wagon hitched to a star. We're not just a feed store, or Western wear, hardware, tack, hous wares, lawn and garden or gifts, we' all of that and more. Someone here even knows how to custom shape hats, kill fire ants, thread pipes and season cast iron. Callahan's Genera Store; 501 Bastrop Hwy.; 512-385-3452; www.callahansgs.com

CHINATOWN CENTE

Chinatown Center is Austin's Fi and Only! With 180,000 squa feet of retail space developed by T. International Group, visitors w find M.T. Supermarket, the large Central Texas Asian supermark authentic Asian restaurants, jewel stores, the Austin Asian America Chamber of Commerce, and over retail shops. Mon.- Sun. 9a.m.-9 p. Store and restaurant hours may va Chinatown Center; 10901 N. Lam 512-343-3688; www.chinatownausti com

COWBOY COOL

Dubbed the "Neiman Marcus western wear," this hip 2nd Street sho is making guys and girls look, we cool. A wide selection of custom-ma boots, shirts, belts and one of a ki accessories you can't find anywhe They can also custom design whatev style of boots you desire. 217 We Second St., Austin TX., 512-70 9000, www.cowboycool.com

(Continued on Page 96)

CRYSTAL WORKS

Delights the eye and soothes the spirit, providing a unique gift-shopping experience. Featuring 14kt and sterling jewelry handcrafted by local jewelers, and spotlighting crystals, fountains, Feng Shui items, music, harmonically tuned wind chimes, aromatherapy products and spiritual reminders. An Austin original for 27 years. Crystal Works; 908 A W. 12th St.; 512-327-0404.

THE DOMAIN

Austin's most fashionable retail destination. The Domain, features seventy-five of the world's most desired retailers, including Neiman Marcus and Macy's, extraordinary restaurants and high-end living space. Visit www. simon.com for a complete retailer listing. The Domain, where luxury lives. 11410 Century Oaks Terrace; 512.795.4230

DREYFUS ANTIQUES

Historic selection of 18th- and 19th-century armoires, wood tables, hutches, leather armchairs, tapestries, decorative architectural pieces and large inventory of light fixtures. George Dreyfus' travel in France provides a collection of country French antiques. Unmatched array and exact replica of the Eiffel Tower. Mon.-Sat. 10 a.m.-6 p.m. Dreyfus Antiques; 1901 N. Lamar Blvd.; 512-473-2443; www.dreyfusantiques.com

EL INTERIOR

With treasures of Mexico for the discerning taste, the store has been an Austin institution since 1979. Exceptional folk art and amazing selection of handwoven textiles and timeless cotton clothing. Includes woodcarvings, silver jewelry, pottery and tin work. Mon.-Sat. 10 a.m. to 6 p.m.; Sun. noon to 5 p.m. El Interior; www.elinterior.com

GARDEN ROOM

One of Austin's most enchanting stores. Creative décor and an appealing mix of unique merchandise delight your senses. Unique clothing and gift items range from the classical to the whimsical. Choose from a myriad of carefully selected accessories – shoes, jewelry, evening bags, hair ornaments and much more. Mon-Sat, 10am – 5:30pm. Garden Room; 1601 W 38th Street; 512-458-5407; www.gardenboomboutique.com

LAKELINE MALL

Home to Dillard's, JCPenney, Macy's, Sears and more than 150 specialty stores, a 9-screen theatre, and a Food Court featuring dazzling architecture! Visit www. simon.com for list of retailers and special events. Conveniently located at US 183 and RR 620 in the northwest sector of Austin, Texas. 11200 Lakeline Mall Drive; 512.257.SHOP.

LOFTY DOG

Pets, tired of the same old shopping grounds? Need a uniquely Austin pet experience? Then ask your human companions to bring you to Lofty Dog, located at 403 W. 2nd Street, where you'll find a huge selection of dog and cat toys, collars, bedding, clothing, locally-made goods, super premium and raw foods, and so much more. For information on free parking hours and locations check out our website at www.austinloftydog.com; 512-476-5050

NOMADIC NOTIONS

With hundreds of beads, you can mix and match from an assortment of glass, wood, bone, gemstone and metal from the four corners of the earth. Relaxed atmosphere and friendly staff, who can provide tips and suggestions on how to create your own piece. Also sell jewelry by local artisans. Nomadic Notions; 3010 W. Anderson Ln.; 512-454-0001

PRIME OUTLETS SAN MARCOS

Texas' largest outlet mall offers over 130 top brand name designer outlets. Just 30 minutes south of Austin, the center is conveniently located off IH-35 at exit 200-Center Point Road. Enjoy Mediterranean architecture and lush green courtyards as you shop and save up to 70%. Prime Outlets; 3939 IH-35 S.; 512-396-2201; www.primeoutlets.com

(Continued on Page 100)

The most artfully-wrapped package of all, should be you.

SHOPPING

FOR OVER 75 YEARS NOW, TEXAS HATTERS HAS BEEN HANDCRAFTING FELT AND PANAMA HATS FOR EVERYONE FROM THE PRINCE OF WALES, FIVE U.S. PRESIDENTS, CONGRESSMEN, SENATORS, COUNTRY, ROCK AND BLUES STARS, TO WORKING COWBOYS, DOCTORS, BANKERS, LAWYERS, JUDGES AND ALL SORTS OF FINE FOLKS.

TAKING A TRIP TO VISIT TEXAS HATTERS IS WELL WORTH THE DRIVE (ROUGHLY 30 MILES SOUTH OF HIGHWAY 183 FROM MLK BLVD. IN AUSTIN) TO SEE VOLUMES OF OLD PHOTOS AND THE HAT HALL OF FAME. YOU CAN TAKE A WINDOW TOUR TO WATCH THE HATS BEING MADE AND IF IT ISN'T TOO BUSY, YOU MIGHT BE LUCKY ENOUGH TO GET A CLOSE-UP AND PERSONAL LOOK-SEE.

TEXAS HATTER'S HOURS ARE TUESDAY THROUGH SATURDAY, 9:30AM TO 5:30PM. CALL AHEAD IF YOU PLAN ON A TOUR, JUST TO MAKE SURE SOMEONE IS AROUND. 800-421-4287. IF YOU CAN'T MAKE THE TRIP, BE SURE TO LOG ON TO WWW.TEXASHATTERS.COM FOR THE HISTROY OF THIS WONDERFUL TEXAS LEGACY AND FOR FUN INFORMATION ON HOW TO MEASURE YOUR HAT SIZE, ON-LINE SHOPPING AND MORE!

GIFTS

CLOTHING

ACCESSORIES

1601 W 38TH ST *at* 5 JEFFERSON SQUARE *in* AUSTIN

(512) 458-5407   *www.gardenroomboutique.com*

MONDAY - SATURDAY 10AM *to* 5:30AM

Treasured SoLa

Just South of the River and between downtown and down South is South Lamar, one of the most treasured streets in Austin. You will feel like an Austinite in this beloved area where oaks stand tall and shade the crooked streets, lined with locals sipping coffee, shopping at vintage stores and cooling off after a bike ride along Town Lake. Spanning from gorgeous Zilker Park all the way down past historic Saxon Pub you will find countless fun ways to pass a lazy Texas weekend in style. Be sure to bring your comfortable shoes- though parking is plentiful, you will find yourself wanting to explore all the delightful nooks and crannys of this beloved area.

(Continued from Page 96)

REWARDS

Rewards is uniquely Austin and features a special blend of merchandise found nowhere else. There are over 400 sterling silver and 14kt gold belt buckles, handmade belts in all sizes and an extensive collection of designer jewelry including pieces by John Atencio, Yvel, Susan Helmich's Angels with Attitudes and hundreds of StoryWheels. Definitely worth a visit. 9722 Great Hills Trail, Suite 300; 512-502-9799; www.shoprewards.com

ROUND ROCK PREMIUM OUTLETS

Discover designer outlet shopping 20 miles north of Austin. Save 25% to 65% every day at 125 stores including Ann Taylor, Banana Republic, BCBG, Max Azria, Burberry, Calvin Klein, Coach, J.Crew, Michael Kors, Nike, Polo Ralph Lauren , Theory and more . Open Mon-Sat 10am-9pm, Sun10am-6pm. For more information, visit www.premiumoutlets.com/roundrock or call (512) 863-6688.

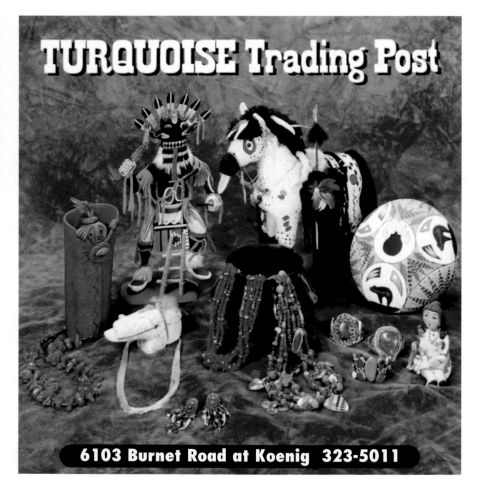

Terra Toys

Terra Toys! Classic, fun, beautiful toys from around the world – intriguing for infant or architect. Children's bookstore, art supplies, science, novelties, candies. Wooden toys, puzzles, games, dolls, miniatures, major plush collection. Landmark store worth the visit. Mon.-Sat., 10 a.m. to 7 p.m.; Sun., noon to 6 p.m. Terra Toys; 2438 W. Anderson Lane; 512-445-4489; www.terratoys.com

Texas Hatters

Hat-making professionals create custom hats to suit the most eclectic of tastes. Texas Hatters "Tops the Best"; some of the people who own one of their famous hats are former President Ronald Reagan, President George W. Bush and Jerry Jeff Walker. Open Tues.-Sat., 9:30 a.m.-5:30 p.m. Texas Hatters; 15755 IH-35 S., Buda; 512-295-4287; www.texashatters.com

Things Celtic

Founded in 1977, this store has the largest selection of Irish and Scottish wedding rings in Texas. Special order handmade kilts from Scotland, American made Utilikilts and rental kilts. Art and unique crafts are featured throughout: jewelry, books, music, candles, pewter and selection of Celtic wall crosses. Open Mon.-Sat., 10 a.m.-6 p.m. and Sun., noon-5 p.m. Things Celtic; 1806 W. 35th St.; 512-472-2358; www.thingsceltic.com

Turquoise Trading Post

Best selection of contemporary and traditional Native American jewelry in Texas. Where Austinites bring their East Coast relatives for gifts to take home. Features Zuni carvings, Navajo kachinas, Pueblo pottery, dream-catchers, carvings, flutes and storytellers, plus distinctive furnishings with a Southwest flair.; 6103 Burnet Rd. at Koenig Ln.; 512-323-5011; www.texasttp.com

Whit Hanks

Austin's premier antiques gallery features extensive collections of European and American antiques and accessories, including furniture, art, silver, lighting, vintage books and rare estate jewelry. Select group of fine antiques merchants attracts the most discriminating and selective dealers and individuals from around the country. Whit Hanks Antiques; 1009 W Sixth St.; 512-478-2101; www.whithanksantiques.com

SHOPPING

Whit Hanks Antiques

A Collection of Fine Antique Galleries

Whit Hanks Antiques is a shopper's paradise, a collector's dream and a designer's resource. Stroll through the galleries of Whit Hanks Antiques and discover why it has earned the prestigious reputation as Austin's premier collection of fine antique galleries.

Antique Swan
Fancy Finds
Halcyon House
House of Lamps and Antiques
Jean-Marc Fray Antiques
JEI Design Collection
Négrel Antiques
Pat Monroe Antiques
1776 House Antiques
Wheeler Antique Silver & Art
Witte Global Antiques

1009 West 6th Street
512-478-2101
whithanksantiques.com

26 Doors Shopping Center:
A Midtown Oasis
1206 W. 38th St.

Whether you're looking for fabulous food, gifts, original toys, or clothing, it can be found at 26 Doors, located in the heart of mid-town Austin.

The shopping center is an Austin original. The central plaza—featuring a bronze sundial—is a perfect meeting place for friends, family and kids. Courtyards feature fountains and beautiful landscaping.

If you're craving a tasty bite to eat, visit SANTA RITA CANTINA, nestled in the heart of 26 Doors. The cantina is a welcoming, casual spot that offers specialties such as fish, salads, and slow-roasted chicken or pork loin, as well as traditional Tex Mex. Be sure to sample their award-winning salsa and famous margaritas. The Cantina has been featured in Rachael Ray's Tasty Travels. Dine indoors or on the large outdoor patio.

ADELANTE BOUTIQUE is a unique women's store with an eclectic mix of clothing, handbags, shoes, and jewelry. Like its name, which means "forward" in Spanish, this boutique is always on the cutting edge, offering the latest style trends.

To satisfy a sweet tooth, treat yourself to TEO'S, a perennial winner of the "Best of Austin" awards. Teo's offers a full-service coffee bar staffed by Italian-trained baristas. Gelato is available in a variety of flavors, and for a refreshing treat, sample a sorbetto. The more than 37 flavors range from an unbelievably creamy chocolate cappuccino gelato called mattissimo to a sugar-free strawberry sorbett They've also added breakfast and lunch menus. In the cool months, enjoy your treats by the outdoor fireplace.

One of Austin's most popular boutiques is SWEE CHARITY, which offers gifts, accessories, seasonal déco collectibles, and art. During the year, Sweet Chari welcomes top designers such as Round Top Collection's Je Krause and chefs like Rebecca Rather and Sibby Barret One of the stores' two signature departments is P.S. b

SANTA ★ RITA
TEX MEX CANTINA

Rootin' Ridge
★ toymakers since 1975

...weet Charity, featuring gifts, cards, and candy. The other, Sweet Baby, offers the
...est in children's attire, toys and furniture. They are a project of Seton Volunteers
...nd proceeds benefit patients in need at Seton.

ROOTIN' RIDGE TOYMAKERS offers custom-made wooden toys for all ages.
...nside, visitors can peek into the workshop to watch the master craftsmen at work.
...Rootin' Ridge also offers a selection of high-quality commercially produced wooden
...oys, games, puzzles, furniture and musical instruments.

Kids feel special when they visit Margo Bower's HAIR'S LAIR. This hair-
...utting and styling salon is located in a small cottage and features toys, movies, and
...nacks. Fast and fabulous hairstyles make kids—and their parents—look forward to
...fun haircut every time. Austin Monthly Magazine named Hair's Lair "Best Kids
...Cut in Austin" in 2006.

THE NEEDLE WORKS specializes in fine, hand-painted canvases and
...n extensive selection of threads. Their collection is exceeded only by their
...ommitment to needlepoint enjoyment: classes, special orders, the latest in
...lesigns and fibers, pulling threads, stitch guides, and finishing.

For a beautiful portrait, make an appointment with NANCY WHITWORTH.
...For more than 20 years, her work has been characterized by natural expression,
...beautiful lighting, and simplicity in design.

Feel more beautiful when you visit URBAN BETTY. The salon offers
...he best and most current trends in professional hair color and styles, as well
...as fabulous updos and wedding treatments—in the salon or at your location.
...Urban Betty features PureOlogy and Bumble & Bumble products.

Pamper yourself at BELLISSIMA EUROPEAN SKIN AND NAILS. Skin care is
...heir passion and life's work. Their methods combine the best of European and
...American skin care techniques and products.

If it's burgers, platters and cold beer that you're searching for, stop by
...WATERLOO ICE HOUSE. Open for breakfast, lunch and dinner, Waterloo is a
...casual neighborhood gathering spot serving great food any time of day. At night,
...he dining room comes alive with the best of Austin's music scene.

From its flagship location in Amarillo, DUNCAN & BOYD JEWELERS has
...served a five-state area for almost 40 years as one of the premier jewelry stores
...n the Southwest. Duncan & Boyd of Austin continues the company tradition of
...providing exceptional quality and personal service.

SHOPPING

Adelante Boutique	512-452-5322	adelanteaustin.com
Bay Hill Designs	512-374-0210	
Bellissima	512-458-4448	bellissimaaustin.com
Duncan & Boyd Jewelers	512-371-7824	duncanboyd.com
Frost Bank	512-473-4391	frostbank.com
Hair's Lair	512-374-1700	
The Needle Works	512-451-6931	theneedleworks.com
RAE Cosmetics	512-320-8732	raecosmetics.com
Rootin' Ridge Toymakers	512-453-2604	rootinridge.com
Santa Rita Cantina	512-419-7482	santaritacantina.com
Sweet Charity	512-451-5375	sweetcharitygifts.org
Teo	512-451-9555	caffeteo.com
Urban Betty	512-371-7663	urbanbetty.com
Waterloo Ice House	512-451-5245	waterlooicehouse.com
Nancy Whitworth	512-451-8331	nancywhitworth.com

Your Address Magazine Luxury Get-Away

Imagine a romantic weekend get-away in the rustic forests of Washington State. No traffic lights, no smog, the moon and the stars wink at you through the gentle undulations of the firs in the peace of the forest. Nestled at the foot of the scenic, snow-capped Mt. Adams, this hide-a-way is a charming, one-of-a-kind tree-house. This special vacation available exclusively through *Your Address Magazine.*

The Inspiration Gift Box

Hand-crafted by Portland artist She's Gifted, each gift box is a unique piece of art decorated with empowering symbols that represent life, creativity, love and more. These boxes make wonderful gifts or decorations, and each one comes with a description of the boxes' symbolic meaning.

On-line Shopping!

Unique items from local artisans and national vendors are available at www.youraddressmagazine.com. We invite you to get on-line and shop!

Chocolates by Bissinger

Bissinger's offers you some of the world's finest handmade, gourmet chocolate. This impressive selection includes boxed chocolates, sugar free chocolate and classic gourmet candies. They also offer an extensive selection of holiday chocolates, chocolate truffles, chocolate covered fruits and more.

Teas and Treats by Bissinger

Enjoy these wildly popular all-natural snacks for any age with the light taste of Pomegranate White Tea Gummy Pandas or the hint of subtle spiced peach and healthful antioxidants with Green Tea Gummy Pandas. A wide selecton of teas and candies available.

Ruby Jane CD

Amazing chid prodigy Ruby Jane will fiddle her way into your heart with her powerful vocals and amazing Southern melodies.

Celebrate

When You Feel the Need to Explore

Sometimes we all want to get away from the commotion of the city, and the best way to do that in Central Texas is to escape to the Hill Country.

BY BRANDON RENNER

Austin is one of the most vibrant and energetic cities in Texas with enough nightlife, restaurants and shopping to keep you satisfied. But sometimes, we all want to get away from the commotion of the city, and the best way to do that in Central Texas is to escape to the hill country. Drive just a few miles outside the city limits, and you'll be in the heart of the slow, easy pace of hill country living.

Made up of most of Austin's surrounding area, the Hill Country offers picturesque views of wildflowers, rugged limestone cliffs and blue skies that go on forever. And there's always something to do around here. You'll find reservoir lakes that are very popular attractions in the area throughout the year. Some of these glistening lakes include Lake LBJ, Lake Buchanan, Lake Marble Falls and Inks Lake. All of them provide an opportunity for water sports like wakeboarding and kayaking and of course, relaxation. For a more active getaway, take a trip outside the city to one of the many state parks and wildlife preserves in the area. There's Enchanted Rock state park, Pedernales Falls and Bastrop State Park, just to name a few. You can go camping, hiking and biking all while catching a glimpse of unique Texas wildlife.

Central Texans always know how to relax and have a good time inside as well. On your tour of the Texas Hill Country, check out one of many tasty little restaurants that dot the area. For an enjoyable night, take a trip out to a classic small town dancehall or camp out beneath the big Texas stars. Like the old song goes, "the stars at night are big and bright, deep in the heart of Texas!" For those who enjoy shopping, there are many quaint and unique boutiques for antiques, fashions, home décor and the like.

Just east of Austin lie the towns of Elgin, Bastrop and Shiner. Elgin is home to many well-known barbeque and sausage joints; Bastrop is peppered with the loblolly pine, a unique area of isolated pines; Shiner is famous for it's Shiner Bock beer, brewed right in the heart of the city.

So when the everyday humdrum of great live music, fantastic restaurants and easy-going Austin culture leaves you cold, it's nice to escape, even if it's only for a day. The only thing that's better than spending a day in Austin is spending a day doing all the things that the surrounding area has to offer.

Top 5 Incentives to Take a Day Trip

2 THE HISTORY
The Texas Hill Country is full of unique legends, tall tal
and interesting history. The history of the Hill Country
the history of Texas.

3 THE SMALL TOWNS
Our region of Texas is made of lots of unique small
towns, just like the ones you've seen in the movies. Visit
some of the old world European settlements in our area
that are over 150 years old.

1 THE VIEW
With rugged limestone hills and
beautiful Texas flora and fauna, the
views of the Texas Hill Country will
be etched in your memory long after
you leave the area.

4 The Wine
The Texas Hill Country has become a huge force in
the wine industry over the past few years. With over a
dozen wineries in the area, a tasting tour will surely in-
troduce your palette to the special flavor of Texas wine.

5 THE FOOD
In such a diverse state, you're sure to find lots of brand
new tastes! Try some spicy enchiladas at one of the
many local Tex-Mex restaurants, a chicken fried steak
at a down home café or grab some fresh fruit from a
roadside stand.

Just a Day Trip Away

DESTINATIONS

ROUND TOP, TX

From car classics to classical music, dining and
"darn" good pies, Round Top has it all. Only 75
minutes from Austin, you can enjoy a day away
any day of the year! Weekend shopping, music
and arts, over 60+ B&B's and historical sites and
tours. Round Top Chamber of Commerce: 979-
249-4042; 888-368-4783; www.roundtop.org

SHINER'S SPOETZL BREWERY

The Spoetzl Brewery, Texas'
oldest independent brewery,
was first established by Czech
and German immigrants as the
"Little Brewery" in Shiner, Texas
in 1909. To satisfy their need
for Old World-tasting brews,
they hired Kosmos Spoetzl, a
Bavarian brew-master whose

traditional family recip
and expertise remain tl
inspiration for the Shir
beers today. Embark on
a historical journey and
savor some of the natio
greatest tasting beers w
a visit to the famous Li
Brewery, located at 603
East Brewery Street in
Shiner. Brewery tours a
available Monday throu
Friday at 11 a.m. and 1:3
p.m. or by special arrangemen
for groups of 20 or more (call
361-594-3383 or 800-5Shiner
The brewery is closed on
weekends and major holidays.
For more information, call 80
5Shiner or visit www.shiner.co
where you can also visit the or
line tour of the Shiner Factory

Don't Forget!

Traveling Essentials

CAMERA – With so many picturesque landscapes in the Texas Hill Country, you will find photo opportunities everywhere you turn. Make sure you have plenty of film or digital memory space to capture the moment.

CANTEEN – Staying hydrated is vital to any hill country getaway. Be sure to bring as much water as you can comfortably carry. Depending on the length of your hike, you should bring at least three quarts per person, per day. Leave at least a gallon of water in your vehicle so that you'll have a fresh water supply upon your return.

SNACKS – Healthy meals are essential to sustain yourself on your trip. Consider a European-style lunch with bread, cheese, hard meats and fruit that doesn't require refrigeration. Of course, energy bars are always a reliable source of relatively long-lasting sustenance.

SUNSCREEN – Lather on generous amounts of sunscreen witih an SPF of no less than 30. As easy as it is to prevent sun damage, it is simply impractical not to take the proper measures.

RELIABLE FOOTWEAR – It is never a good idea to bring new shoes on a hike. Bring comfortable hiking boots or athletic shoes that have been properly broken in, and couple them with high quality socks that will withstand the mileage.

BATHING SUIT – Central Texas is a veritable treasure trove of natural lakes, rivers, creeks and springs that are perfect for taking a refreshing dip after a fulfilling hike. Be prepared to fully enjoy a rejuvenating escape that Mother Nature provides.

BUG REPELLANT – We have to share our beautiful hill country with plenty of creepy crawlers with toxins that are harmful to our health. Show them they are not welcome by liberally applying bug repellant to clothing,

paying special attention to your shoes and socks.

TRASH BAGS – Be sure to keep nature as beautiful as you find it. Take your waste back with you, and keep it far away from trails and water sources.

ADVERTISING INDEX

III Forks...13
2nd Street District................................11
3 Graces Spa.......................................49
3 White Doves.....................................MF-5
26 Doors Shopping Center.................104, 105
Ah-Ha..MF-5
Airscape Parasail...................................21
All My Sons...60
Allens Boot....................................Back Cover
Amelia's Retrovogue & Relics.................100
Ancient Way Day Spa............................46
Arabic Bazaar......................................21
The Arboretum....................................97
Art on 5th..41
Artworks..43
As You Like It Interiors.........................MF-5
Austin Carriage Services........................22
Austin Duck Adventures........................22
Austin Gay & Lesbian Int'l Film Fest..........20
Austin Gift Company.............................18
Austin Land & Cattle............................80
Austin Polo Club..................................34
Baby Face Salon & Day Spa....................47
Barton Creek/Lakeline Mall.....................2
Bead It...100
Benihana...80
Bluebonnet Café.................................MF-8
Bobalu..22
Cafe Blué..6
Callahan's..93
Cantina Laredo....................................77
Carlos'N Charlie's...................................6
Carmelo's......................................82, 83
Casino el Camino.................................66
Charge d'affaires Concierge.....................59
Chinatown Center.................................19
Cookies by Design.................................55
Cool River..77
The County Line BBQ............................79
Cowboy Cool...7
Coyote Ugly Saloon...............................67
Crystal Works......................................101
Doc's MotorWorks................................87
The Domain...1
Dreyfus Antiques..................................95
Eastside Café...................................76, 88
El Gallo...78
El Interior..96
Electric Cars of Austin...........................21
Estância Churrascaría...............................9
Falconhead Golf...............................31, 37
The Flower Studio.................................53
Frank & Angie's....................................86
The Garden Room.................................99
GG Ganache......................................MF-4
Golf Club at Grey Rock...........................37
Golf Club at Star Ranch..........................37
Horseshoe Bay Corporation.......HSB-9, HSB-12
Horseshoe Bay Resort at the Marriott......HSB-1, HSB-16

Horseshoe Bay Resort............................HSB-13
Hut's Hamburgers.................................86
Iguana Grill..30
Iron Cactus..6
Just For Fun..6
Kathy Womack Gallery...........................42
Lady Bird Wildflower Center....................21
Lights 'n Such.....................................MF-5
Lone Star Riverboats.............................21
Lorraine's Live Music Venue....................MF-6
Lucky Lizard/ Museum of the Weird...........22
Maggie Mae's......................................65
Marble Falls/Lake LBJ Chamber of Commerce.......MF-7
ME Television......................................71
The Melting Pot...................................85
Mesa Ranch..81
Nomadic Notions..................................98
The OASIS.....................................23-28
Onion Creek Salon & Spa........................47
Out Back Unlimited..............................MF-5
Pete's Piano Bar...................................66
Playa Management, LLC.........................111
PPD..61
Prime Outlets San Marcos........................3
Randy Smith, Ltd..................................40
Remax Horseshoe Bay..........................HSB-22
Renaissance Austin/Banderas...................89
Rewards.....................Inside Front Cover, 102
Rick's Cabaret.....................................72
River City Grille...................................MF-8
Round Rock Premium Outlets...................93
Round Top Chamber..............................110
Ruth's Chris Steak House.........................78
Salem's Jewelry...................................MF-1
Saxon Pub..68
Schlitterbahn......................................4, 5
Shiner...69, 110
Skywater Over Horseshoe Bay......HSB-2, HSB-3
Solid Gold Boutique. Day Spa...............46, 98
Star of India.......................................78
Starlite...81
Terra Toys/Dragonsnaps!.........................92
Texas Hatters......................................98
Texas Hill Country Wineries........Inside Back Cover
Texas Memorial Museum.........................22
Texas Military Forces Museum...................18
Texas Ski Ranch...................................36
Things Celtic.......................................101
Tito's Handmade Vodka..........................70
Tree House Italian Grill...........................83
Turquoise Trading Post..........................100
Until.org..35
Villa dal Lago....................................HSB-24
Volente Beach/Blu Parrot.........................29
Waterloo Ice House...............................87
Whit Hanks Antiques.............................103
Yellow Rose...73
Your Address Magazine.............8, 17, 106, 107
Zinger Hardware...................................22

ALTITUDE ENHANCES ATTITUDE.

The Marriott Hotel at Horseshoe Bay Resort offers 51,000 sq. ft. of indoor & outdoor event space which is centrally located. The hotel features 349 guest rooms including 18 suites. Guests may take advantage of resort amenities including 14 tennis courts, 3 Robert Trent Jones Sr. golf courses, 18 hole par 72 Whitewater putting course, 3 Whirlpools, 4 Pools, Bayside Spa & Fitness Center, Hill Country Dining, Full Service Marina with Watercraft Rentals and Lake LBJ.

866-799-5384
www.horseshoebaymarriott.com

HORSESHOE BAY RESORT
TEXAS HILL COUNTRY
Marriott.

yourTexas

Your best drives come with commanding views. With Lake LBJ and Horseshoe Bay at hand, you will soon experience our new Jack Nicklaus Signature Golf Course—where heroes are made.

Skywater. **Discover your Texas in every direction.**

skywatertexas.com | 888.548.2551

HILL COUNTRY LUXURY HOMESITES FROM THE 200s
OPPORTUNITY FOR EXCLUSIVE HORSESHOE BAY RESORT MEMBERSHIP
JACK NICKLAUS SIGNATURE GOLF COURSE UNDER CONSTRUCTION
LEED CERTIFIED APPROACH
PRIVATE JET CENTER, YACHT CLUB & MARINA

A Signature Golf Course

N

PRIVATE FLIGHT HOME

W

EAGLE ON #14

BURGERS AT THE CLUB

E

S

ROUNDS WITH DAD

SKYWATER
OVER HORSESHOE BAY

Skywater Over Horseshoe Bay is listed by Skywater Realty—a DMB Realty Company {www.dmbrealty.com}.

Welcome to
Horseshoe Bay Resort

Welcome to one of the most beautiful and luxurious resorts in Texas. Horseshoe Bay Resort, recognized by Golf Digest, Southern Living, Texas Highways, Texas Monthly, The New York Times and many other reputable publications as a place worthy of a much-needed getaway in the Texas Hill Country. The sights, sounds and tastes of Horseshoe Bay Resort will energize your spirit and linger in your mind long after you have returned home to the hectic work world.

You'll want to come back again and again, and perhaps end up staying for a lifetime in your new waterfront home or condominium. The three championship golf courses are first-class, the state-of-the-art spa and fitness center are superb, the gourmet fare is unforgettable, and the Hill Country views are spectacular. Located on the southern shore of Lake LBJ, an estimated 45-minute drive from Austin, Horseshoe Bay Resort is conveniently positioned in the heart of Central Texas.

You deserve only the best to vacation, or live, in a place that rejuvenates your mind, body and soul. One of the most highly sought-after Texas vacation destinations is waiting for you – Horseshoe Bay Resort.

The History of
Horseshoe Bay Resort

Once known as Texas' best kept secret, Horseshoe Bay Resort now receives rave reviews from travel and golf writers such as Joe Passov, architecture/course ranking editor for Golf Magazine. In 2005, he proclaimed Horseshoe Bay Resort one of "America's Best Golf Resorts" and bestowed it with the prestigious Silver Medal award.

It all began with a grand vision in 1971 Horseshoe Bay founders, Norman and Wayne Hurd, wanted to create a world-class destination resort where the hills and lakes converged harmoniously. A short drive from Austin, the new getaway haven on Lake LBJ consisted of The Yacht Club, one 18-hole golf course and a 6,000-foot airstrip.

In 1996, Morris Douglas Jaffe, Jr. acquired 100% ownership of the Resort. Jaffe shared the dream of Horseshoe Bay's original founders, and through years of dedication to impeccable elegance and excellence in customer service, produced the luxurious Horseshoe Bay Resort. The resort has grown to include three Robert Trent Jones, Sr. championship golf courses, three stunning swimming pools, a white sand beach, state-of-the-art spa and fitness facility, full-service marina, three first-class restaurants, twelve professional tennis courts, a beautifully landscaped putting course and a three hundred and forty nine-room Marriott Hotel. The Jet Center provides the ultimate in convenience and efficiency for resort members with private planes.

These grand additions to the Resort move travel writers to sing its praises. "When I look out on the silvery waters of the lake, I feel like asking the same question that ballplayer asked in the movie Field of Dreams: 'Is this heaven?'" writes Les Thomas, Southern Living (August 2006). Offering the highest level of customer service is only the beginning of Horseshoe Bay Resort's promise to remain the premier resort destination in Texas. Douglas Jaffe, III, took the helm as CEO in 2004 with a fervor for excellence and a penchant for innovative ideas for the Resort.

"Horseshoe Bay Resort is a place of passion: passion for life, for beauty and for the serenity of the Texas Hill Country. Passion for family and friendship and a sense of community and for everything that makes for a fulfilling life. I am confident that generations of families will continue creating some of their fondest memories at Horseshoe Bay Resort, just as my family and I have over the years," says Douglas Jaffe, III.

More than thirty five years have been invested in the planning, creation, and development of Horseshoe Bay Resort, the premier Resort community in Texas.

"When people talk about Central Texas becoming America's third coast, they are undoubtedly referring to the opulent lifestyle at Horseshoe Bay Resort. With a world-renowned yacht club, a white sand beach and a cool breeze drifting in from Lake LBJ, (Central Texas' largest constant-level lake) the properties and amenities of Horseshoe Bay make you wonder if six stars should be the new standard," writes Chris Kocek, Austin Home and Living (July, 2006).

Choose Your Lifestyle

HORSESHOE BAY®

- ◆ **Breathtaking Views**
- ◆ **Constant Level Lake**
- ◆ **Incredible Golf**
- ◆ **Gated Communities**
- ◆ **Superb Real Estate**

Horseshoe Bay Corp

P.O. Box 7752, Horseshoe Bay, Texas 78657

www.horseshoebay.com

800-292-1545   830-598-2553

Accommodations

Horseshoe Bay Resort offers luxury, comfort and impeccable service to members and guests. That is why more than 100,000 visitors each year choose this beautiful setting for their special getaway and many end up calling it home.

The Marriott Hotel and Conference Center's 349 guest rooms, including 117 suites, offer panoramic views of Lake LBJ and the legendary Texas Hill Country. From the moment you check into Marriott's first Resort Hotel in the state, you will discover tranquility.

You won't have to go far to enjoy all of the hotel's wonderful amenities, such as the 24-hour fitness center or The Market, where Starbucks and Ben and Jerry's Ice Cream await you. Lantana Grill and Bar, the 44th restaurant opened by David Blossom, a level one sommelier, offers scrumptious dining options for breakfast, lunch and dinner.

Pets and young adults are welcome at the Hill Country Marriott Hotel at Horseshoe Bay Resort. The concierge is ready to make reservations for your children to join the action-packed adventures available through Monarch Kid's Club or to point the way to bicycle rentals to explore the incredible landscape of Horseshoe Bay Resort.

The hotel also caters to business travelers and large groups. The Business Center is available 24 hours a day, seven days a week.

Adjacent to the Marriott Hotel are 100 Paseo Condos with one-, two-, and three-bedroom units available with spa tubs. Guests of the hotel or any of the Resort-owned condos can experience full access to all Horseshoe Bay Resort has to offer, whether it's playing a challenging round on one of the three championship golf courses, or taking in a magnificent sunset on the Yacht Club deck.

Horseshoe Bay Resort teamed up with Centex Destination Properties to unveil its latest offering in Resort accommodations. Unit owners at The Waters at Horseshoe Bay Resort are given the opportunity to participate in a resort-managed rental program. The Waters at Horseshoe Bay Resort brings a long-awaited luxury mid-rise offering to visitors. These new units, located near the Resort's white sand beach and the crystal blue waters of Lake LBJ, provide guests with options like never before. Whether owners wish to make their unit available for rent for just a few months a year, or all but three weeks, the choice is theirs.

"Horseshoe Bay Resort Real Estate continues to benefit from national real estate trends, maintaining steady sales of traditional golf course and view homes and complemented by a strong, appreciating waterfront market. As an illustration to the growth of the area, Horseshoe Bay now boasts many new and exciting residential developments including The Trails of Lake LBJ, Siena Creek and The Waters at Horseshoe Bay Resort, each with its own distinct personality and unique residential opportunities," says Mike Gordon, director of real estate operations. Imagine sitting on your deck at The Waters, drinking in the view of Texas' largest constant-level lake, Lake LBJ, or the panorama of colorful Hill Country flowers. Thoughts of the rapid-paced world left behind will soon disappear as you prepare for the vacation of a lifetime. Once you sample the premier lifestyle offered at Horseshoe Bay Resort, you'll want to come back again and again.

[*come play*]

HORSESHOE BAY
RESORT

www.hsbresort.com

The most luxurious and comprehensive playground is waiting for you when it's time to rejuvenate your spirit. This dream destination is Horseshoe Bay Resort, located in the very heart of Texas, less than an hour from Austin. Lake LBJ's cool waters stretch for miles from the Resort's shoreline and, as the largest constant-level lake in the state, Lake LBJ will never lose its impressive, dramatic view. Living at the Resort or sampling this amazing lifestyle for a weekend is simply heaven.

Horseshoe Bay Resort offers so many world-class recreational opportunities you'll have a hard time deciding what to do first. Sitting on the deck of your villa at The Waters, drinking in the lake and hill country landscape or walking the impeccably landscaped Resort grounds are favorite pastimes of members and guests. The Resort boasts three championship Robert Trent Jones, Sr. golf courses, a one-of-a-kind, par 72 "golf in miniature" putting course featuring Bermuda grass, a state-of-the-art spa and fitness facility, a full-service marina, three first-class restaurants, 12 professional tennis courts, three stunning swimming pools, a white sand beach and a 349-room Hill Country Marriott Hotel.

Another benefit setting Horseshoe Bay Resort apart from all others is the Jet Center. Where else can you land your private plane and tee off just moments later?

Last year, several national golf publications recognized Horseshoe Bay Resort and its championship golf courses. Golf Digest's "Best Places to Play" gave the Apple Rock, Ram Rock and Slick Rock golf courses four and a half stars. The Resort received the Silver Medal Award from Golf Magazine and Ram Rock and Apple Rock golf courses made the "Top 15 Courses in Texas" according to Golfweek.

"Three challenging courses— Ram Rock, Apple Rock and Slick Rock—careen through the hills. There are 82 sand traps and water hazards on just 12 of the holes on Slick Rock, and it's the most forgiving. Ram Rock often wins the vote for the most difficult course in Texas," writes Les Thomas in Southern Living (August 2006).

Come see for yourself. You will want to experience firsthand the satisfaction of a perfect swing that sends your golf ball flying over the Resort's well-manicured greens. Under the care of Chris Rather, the Resort's new director of golf course agronomy, you can be assured of only the finest golfing experience. Rather previously held superintendent positions with Buffalo Creek Golf Club, Lake Arlington Golf Course, Riverhill Country Club, and before joining Horseshoe Bay Resort, served as director of agronomy at Boot Ranch in Fredericksburg. Golf course architect Robert Trent Jones, Sr., designed an estimated 500 prestigious courses during his lifetime. His three creations for Horseshoe Bay Resort are among his finest works of art. The pro shops and full-service clubhouses carry the latest in international golf fashions, equipment and personalized gift items. You can shop, dine, and catch up with friends all under one roof.

The Resort has made it even more convenient to play golf for out-of-town members who fly personal or business planes. The Jet Center features a 6,000-foot runway that can accommodate aircrafts as large as a Regional Jetliner, and comes equipped with a luxury lounge and resort transportation. Whether you plan a quick golf getaway or a longer stay, you'll be provided with a safe, luxurious landing.

The weather at Horseshoe Bay Resort, with an average annual temperature of 69 degrees, is ideal for golfing, boating, tennis or poolside family gatherings nearly year round. Soak up the sun as you relax on the beautiful white sand beaches, or just steps away, plunge into the outdoor lagoon-size pool. The Resort's one-of-a-kind volcanic rock hot tub can accommodate you and 26 of your closest friends.

If boating is your preference during your time at Horseshoe Bay Resort, the lake and marina are for you. Enjoy 23 miles of constant, clear water as you motor across the shimmering surface. All members of your family can enjoy the lake through the rental of waverunners, pontoon boats and other water sports equipment. The Resort also offers fishing tours and boat storage facilities.

Pampering yourself is a prerequisite at Horseshoe Bay Resort. It's time to treat yourself to a day at the state-of-the-art, full-service Bayside Spa and Fitness Center.

WE NOW PRONOUNCE YOUR WEDDING BREATHTAKING.

Planning a day this special shouldn't be left up to just anyone. But rather, someone you can trust. At the Horseshoe Bay Resort Marriott you'll be assured as to our dedication of providing you the wedding of your dreams.

With both generous and elegant spaces in our ballroom, and unique and inviting outdoor spaces throughout the resort, your fairy tale wedding is just a call away. An array of amenities awaits guests as well, such as golf, tennis, and spa excursions. Experience gracious service, personalized catering and both spacious and stylish guestrooms.

For more information contact our Sales and Catering Department at 800-452-5330 or visit Horseshoebaymarriott.com

HORSESHOE BAY RESORT
TEXAS HILL COUNTRY

Marriott.

"Personal trainers are also available to customize an exercise program that's just right for you."

Features include steam rooms, sauna and whirlpools, and a long list of soothing spa services—facials, massages and nail treatments—guaranteed to make you sigh with pleasure. Bayside's signature body indulgence includes a combination of body treatments. Begin with an exfoliating body scrub to reveal the healthiest of skin, followed by a moisture mask containing a mixture of hydrating essential oils, and finish off with an aromatherapy massage allowing for complete and total relaxation.

If you want to pump things up, the Aerobics Hall offers lo-impact, step, strength training and Pilates classes. Personal trainers are also available to customize an exercise program that's just right for you.

Tennis enthusiasts are not forgotten either at the Resort. The Tennis Center, featuring 12 Laykold, Clay and Pro-Grass courts, includes racket rental, ball machines, lighted courts for night play, and private tennis instruction upon request. Your children will love the Monarch Kids Club, full of arts, crafts and games for ages four to 12, available at the Hill Country Marriott Hotel at Horseshoe Bay Resort.

Dining

The tantalizing smells from Horseshoe Bay Resort's four restaurants will greet you long before the mouth-watering selections hit your tongue. Whether you are looking for a casual or formal atmosphere, a table with a lakeside or golf course view, or the opportunity to sample Oysters Rockefeller or Chicken Alfredo, there is a dining option for you at the Resort.

In May of 2006, CEO Douglas Jaffe, III, and staff welcomed Executive Chef John LaFond to its impressive team of professionals. LaFond comes with a list of credentials to wow even the most discriminating taste buds. Previously, LaFond was executive chef at Canyons Ski Resort in Park City, Utah, and Bishop's Lodge in Sante Fe, New Mexico.

"His work at the Yacht Club brings a stylish complexity to the palate in such goodies as...a burly double-cut pork chop, graced with roasted shallots and Swiss chard," writes June Naylor, Texas Highways Magazine (August 2006).

The Yacht Club has been the anchor restaurant at Horseshoe Bay Resort for more than 30 years. You can almost hear the clinking wine glasses and the laughter of celebrations and traditions of years past as you enter the warm, elegant dining room. The Yacht Club's reputation for elegant lakeside dining is unsurpassed. The staff prepares its food with meticulous care and attention to detail. Who could resist sampling the flavors of the Mediterranean Bouillabaisse, Grilled Tuna Rossini or Colorado Rack of Lamb? And after you've been treated to one of these superb entrees, accompanied by a crisp salad, you will surely want to save room for one of the decadent desserts.

In the center of the Yacht Club, you'll find The Y Bar, the essence of sophistication and glamour. The sleek surroundings, with high-back leather booths and soft lighting, offer a cozy atmosphere in which to enjoy an after-dinner cocktail and an aromatic cigar. The Y Bar is the perfect daytime or nighttime getaway to spend with your special someone or a group of friends watching the home game on one of the two large, flat-screen plasma televisions.

Before you tee off, stop in for a hearty breakfast at either the Cap Rock or Slick Rock Bar and Grill. These eateries are located right by the greens, offering the perfect spot for lunch or early dinner after an enjoyable eighteen holes on one of the three championship golf courses. Both restaurants offer pub fare such as

nachos, wings and onion rings, plus a full bar to quench your thirst. The Cap Rock Bar & Grill's clubhouse is Horseshoe Bay Resort's version of dining in a tower. The design is modeled after the spectacular elevations famous in the Ram Rock and Apple Rock golf courses. Who wouldn't feel the breathtaking energy of Horseshoe Bay Resort's golfing community as you look across the greens from above?

The Slick Rock Bar & Grill's claim to fame is its legendary burger, referred to by many customers as "the best burger in the Austin area." As you sink your teeth into this mouth-watering delight, your eyes can also feast on the fountains, gardens and beautiful fairways before you.

Southwest and Texas Hill Country cuisine unite at the Lantana Grill and Bar

in the Marriott Hotel and Conference Center. Delectable fare, including the signature lavender crème brulee, is prepared with fresh, local ingredients. The breakfast buffet is hailed as the best in the Hill Country. Lunch on the patio promises a tasteful and fulfilling escape. In the evening, the restaurant comes alive with the mantra of fire and spice meals and the choice of more than 200 wines.

Visit The Market at the hotel, open to hotel guests, resort members and the public to savor a creamy pastry and a cappuccino from Starbucks. If in need of reading material, a wide variety of publications is also available at the newsstand. Now you are ready to settle in for some alone time to think about life's pleasures and plans for the rest of the day.

Real Estate

When you purchase a waterfront home, golf course lot or condominium at Horseshoe Bay Resort, you are investing in a world-class resort lifestyle. Nearly 5,000 property owners have discovered the peace of mind that comes after making the smart commitment to live at Texas' most luxurious resort destination, less than an hour away from Austin. Whether you are planning full-time or weekend living at the Resort, your special getaway place will undoubtedly deliver many hours of personal fulfillment and enjoyment.

Mike Gordon, director of real estate operations at Horseshoe Bay Resort, says golf and the water are the main selling benefits for prospective clients who come from all parts of the country and world. The Resort boasts three championship courses designed by Robert Trent Jones, Sr., master golf course architect. Slick Rock, Ram Rock and Apple Rock golf courses frequently make the "Best of" lists in national golf publications. Whitewater, a $3.5 million, par 72 putting course, completes the Resort's excellent options for golfing enthusiasts.

"Lake LBJ is always at a constant level, so waterfront homeowners never lose their gorgeous view," says Gordon. "The water and Hill Country views are what former Texans, who have moved from the state after college or for business, are missing. They eventually come back and choose Horseshoe Bay Resort."

Horseshoe Bay Resort Realty represents an impressive portfolio of different Real Estate opportunities including waterfront, golf course and beautiful Hill Country view homes, town homes and home sites. You can always expect the most professional real estate services and commitment to quality in every phase of your purchase.

The Trails of Lake LBJ boasts miles of shady trees, a full-service equestrian center, a private marina and remarkable views. Owning property here is country living with a resort lifestyle. The Trails of Lake LBJ offers a secure, gated community with miles of private hiking and nature trails. "The highest priority at The Trails of Lake LBJ is master planning to protect homeowner privacy and respecting the spectacular 360-degree Hill Country views," says Gordon.

The Waters at Horseshoe Bay Resort is located in the heart of the Resort, offering second-home living unique to Texas. Luxury villas at The Waters are just steps away from the lapping waters of Lake LBJ and the white sand beach. Telling your friends the lake is right outside your door is no exaggeration. Living in one of the spacious, single-level villas at The Waters also places the world-class amenities of Horseshoe Bay Resort right in your backyard. Residents of The Waters have access to a private pool and hot tub, outdoor barbeque area and pavilion, and shoreline boardwalks. It's a perfect spot for entertaining friends

and family! Dave Caldwell with The New York Times writes, "Many of the newer homes at Horseshoe Bay are stunning; architecture runs the gamut from Mediterranean to Hill Country rustic to contemporary." (May 19, 2006)

We recommend you come see for yourself the beauty and world-class resort lifestyle that await you at Horseshoe Bay Resort.

Horseshoe Bay Resort is a privately owned Resort. In 2004, the hotel was built and Marriott was hired to manage it. Guests of the new Hill Country Marriott Hotel at Horseshoe Bay Resort are granted temporary membership allowing access to the private amenities during their stay in Horseshoe Bay.

All of the Resort's amenities, including the golf courses, tennis courts, pools, beaches, Whitewater putting course, the pro shops, marina, jet center and the spa and fitness center are all owned and managed by the Resort and are not affiliated with Marriott.

RE/MAX Horseshoe Bay Resort Sales Co
(EACH OFFICE INDEPENDENTLY OWNED & OPERATED)

(830)598-8726 or (800)486-8727

www.REMAX-HSB-TX.com

"Marketing the Homes & Homesites of Horseshoe Bay and Lake LBJ."

Horseshoe Bay offers everything you looking for all in one place. Whether you looking for a nice place to retire and relax, or a place where you can enjoy fine amenities, Horseshoe Bay Resort offers everything you are looking for. Nesteled in the heart of Texas, 45 minutes west of Austin, Horseshoe Bay Resort lies along the shores of Lake LBJ. Horseshoe Bay Resort boasts three championship Robert Trent Jones, Sr. golf courses, an 18-hole par 72 Dwarf Bermuda grass putting course, four stunning swimming pools, a white sand beach, a spa and fitness facility, a full-service marina, five dining facilities, 12 professional tennis courts, and a 349-room Horseshoe Bay Resort Marriott Hotel. The Horseshoe Bay Resort Airport and Jet Center includes a terminal building housing a luxury passenger lounge, fueling services, a crew lounge and resort transportation. The 6,000-foot runway is one of the largest private airstrips in the state and can accommodate all personal and business aircraft up to a Regional Jetliner. Once travelers land at the Airport and Jet Center, aircraft parking and hangar spaces are available. **RE/MAX** agents have the experience you can count on to make you real estate dreams come true. No one has more experience with Horseshoe Bay Real Estate and the surrounding area, than our highly trained professional sales staff, who are all licensed Realtors.® Located at 7409 Hwy 2147, our office is open 7-days a week for your convenience.

Nobody in the World Sells more Real Estate than
RE/MAX®

Alwand VAHAN

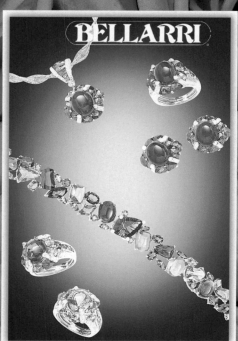

BELLARRI

Simon G.

HEARTS ON FIRE®
THE WORLD'S MOST PERFECTLY CUT DIAMOND®

A. Jaffe
CREATED WITH PASSION SINCE 1892

Salem's
Jewelry
Designer Jewelry & Gifts

Salem's Center
518 Hwy 281
Marble Falls, TX
830-693-2212

Hwy 29 & 281
101 S Water
Burnet, TX
512-756-8748

Celebrate
Marble Falls

LOCATED IN THE HEART OF TEXAS' HILL COUNTRY, MARBLE FALLS IS A SMALL CITY WITH A BIG TEXAS PAST.

BY WHITNEY PRIDDY

Located in the heart of Texas' Hill Country, Marble Falls is a small city with a big Texas past. Marble Falls was named after its legendary series of waterfalls that descended a 22-foot ledge on the Colorado River. In 1951, with the completion of the Max Starcke Dam, the falls became submerged under Lake Marble Falls and are no longer visible. The falls did not survive the change, but Marble Falls lived on and is now a flourishing haven in the hill country with plenty of outdoor adventure and lake activities and a quaint village-like downtown providing amazing opportunities for shopping, dining and Texas fun.

Part of the Highland Lake Chain, which is the largest lake chain in Texas, Lake Marble Falls is the newest and the smallest lake at only 780 acres. The water sits between Lake LBJ to the north and Lake Travis to the south. Water sports are a favorite around town; from swimming to sailing and boating, locals love spending time in the warm Texas sun. Every few years, when the lake is lowered for repair, you can still see the namesake falls that lie beneath. Lake Marble Falls is well known for providing a channel for recreational activity but was originally created to supply hydroelectric power to the growing city.

Fortunate for the locals and visitors who love the Marble Falls outdoors, the Central Texas climate permits ample outdoor activities nearly year-round. With an average summer temperature around 90 degrees and winter temperatures averaging 65 degrees, there are few bad weather days to keep anyone inside. The great weather provides ideal conditions for Lake Fest, Marble Falls' annual August boating festival, which has now been a tradition for 15 years. The Lake Fest races primarily focus on Drag Boats; hosting over 100 boats reaching speeds of over 250 miles per hour can create quite a stir in this town with a population of 5,000. During this festival the population quadruples, bringing people from all parts of Texas.

In addition to water activities, Marble Falls provides plenty of opportunities to enjoy Texas' expansive hill country. There are over 50 acres of parkland located around the area designed for family entertainment. Surround yourself with Oak and Juniper in any of three municipal parks, located on either side of the inlet of Lake Marble Falls, that host a variety of enjoyments including golfing, volleyball courts, picnic areas, swimming, playgrounds, tennis and lakeside views. Much of this area would make a great setting for any outdoor celebration.

Marble Falls is one of 45 cities that are located in the Texas Hill Country. There are several scenic drives that will take you on a lovely tour of the beautiful countryside. Try RM 141, RM 2147 and Texas 71 for views of the northwest and southeast Hill Country and glimpses of the Highland Lakes. The scenic views from these roads are to be remembered.

Marble Falls is proud to be the home of Granite Mountain, a popular site for tourists to visit. It houses the famed pink and red granite that was quarried for the construction of the Texas State Capitol in the 1880's. Though the quarry is off-limits, you can visit the dome shaped mountain and admire its spectacular color.

Longhorn Caverns State Park is a spectacular place to see nature in action; admire the wildlife and to take respite from the hectic activity of city life. This striking park features the famous Longhorn Cavern which hosts tours every day of the week. The cavern has a vivid and rich history, once the home of ice age animals, then to Comanche Indians four centuries ago and up till the Civil War, it was still in use as a Confederate stronghold and the rumored hideout of Texas outlaw Sam Bass. Also nearby find numerous hunting grounds during season.

Be drawn to Marble Falls and take advantage of this expansive and secluded piece of Texas history in the making. Enjoy the breathtaking Hill Country in its finest form. From boating to hunting and shopping to casual dining, Marble Falls has anything you need for a relaxing day trip or even a vacation.

"A DAY IN THE COUNTRY" BY RANDY SMITH (PHOTO LEFT)

Marble Falls

HISTORICAL POINTS OF INTEREST

MARBLE FALLS DEPOT: 801 US 281. Texas Mining and Improvement Company deeded land on Avenue N in Marble Falls for a depot to the Austin and Northwestern railroad. A building was erected on the site in 1893 and was later purchased by the Southern Pacific Railroad. The depot was closed in 1968 and was not used until purchased by a local businessman who donated the structure to the Chamber of Commerce and the City. The old depot was then moved to the present location, restored, and now serves as the Marble Falls/Lake LBJ Chamber of Commerce offices. In 2002, the Chamber hosted a 25th anniversary celebration for the depot's service to visitors in its current location.

GRANITE MOUNTAIN: The historical marker (a granite monolith) is located on RR 1431 on the western edge of town and commemorates the 866-foot dome of solid pink granite. The formation covers 180 acres and contains the largest quarry of its kind in the United States. A special railroad line was built to haul the granite to Austin when the rock was used to build the state Capitol building. The tracks and active quarry activities can be seen from the roadside park on RR 1431.

GOVERNOR O.M. ROBERTS HOME: 819 Seventh Street. Governor Roberts was president of the 1861 Secession Convention and a Confederate officer. He served as governor of Texas from 1879 to 1883, and was later a professor of law at the University of Texas. Roberts settled in this house at Third and Main streets after his retirement in 1893. The structure was later moved to its present location. (Now it is a private residence.)

HILLS OF HOME MEMORIAL: This historical marker commemorates Oscar J. Fox, the famous composer of western tunes such as Get Along Little Doggie. It is located on US 281, on the hillside south of the Colorado River, now overlooking Lake Marble Falls. This is the view that inspired Fox to write his beautiful song, The Hills of Home.

OTTO EBELING HOUSE: 601 Avenue F. Banker Otto Ebeling built this Victorian residence for his wife, Emilie Giesecke, and their four children shortly after moving to Marble Falls. The structure has served as a nursing home, a photographic studio and currently is a private residence.

CHRISTIAN-MATERN HOUSE: 603 7th Avenue. Juliet Johnson Christian, daughter of the founder of Marble Falls, and her husband had this home built in 1892. Ivo B. & Mina Matern bought the house in 1908 and owned it for 51 years. Mr. Matern served as mayor of Marble Falls in 1937.

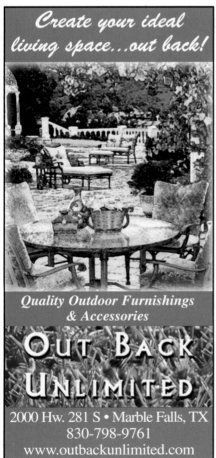

Granite Mountain

BY THE MARBLE FALLS CHAMBER OF COMMERCE

An 866-foot dome of solid pink granite covers 189 acres on the western outskirts of Marble Falls. That dome is called Granite Mountain and is a part of the mineral-rich geological environment called the Llano Uplift. Controlled originally by Comanche Indians, Huge Rock was traded to its first white owners for about two acres of land.

A dispute arose in the 1880s over the type of stone to be used in the construction of the state capitol building in Austin. Governor John Ireland resisted demands to use non-native limestone, and plans to use limestone from Oatmanville (present Oak Hill) had to be canceled when the stone proved to be unfit for exterior use. Granite Mountain's true fame began on July 29, 1885, when the owners donated to the people of Texas, granite sufficient and suitable for the building, erection and completion of the entire State Capitol Building. Convict labor was contracted for the tremendous task of cutting the granite into blocks for shipping. Mule-drawn flat cars were used to haul the blocks to the dressing and shaping grounds at the quarry. A narrow gauge railroad was specifically built to haul the 15,700 carloads of granite from the quarry to the Capitol Building site in Austin. The Texas Capitol is second in size only to the National Capitol. When constructed, it was said to be the seventh largest building in the world.

Granite from Granite Mountain was used in the construction of many buildings known for their beautiful design, such as the Georgia Pacific Building and the Coca-Cola Building both in Atlanta; and the Crocker Building in San Francisco. It was also used for the famed Galveston, Texas, seawall and virtually every jetty on the Texas gulf coast.

Although quarrying has continued for almost 100 years, the size of the huge mass has changed very little. Centuries worth of granite are left in the quarry, which is the largest of its kind in the United States.

Granite Mountain was born more than 4.5 billion years ago when the earth's surface was just forming. Granite is a stone that is composed of quartz, feldspar, and usually mica. Properly installed, it should last forever.

Granite Mountain was purchased by Cold Spring Granite Company, of Cold Spring, Minn., in 1951, and has operated under the name Texas Granite Corp. since that time. Texas Granite Corp. is the world's largest fabricator of granite products, including interior and exterior structural granite, landscape and industrial granite, and memorials.

Calender of Events 2007

JANUARY 1
WALKWAY OF LIGHTS
This is the last opportunity to enjoy over 1 million lights in Lakeside Park. This holiday wonderland will be open from 6:00 pm to 10:00 (weather permitting).

MARCH 8
MARKET DAY
More than 100 vendors with a variety of items, 9:00 am to 4:00 pm. Location: Main Street

APRIL 12
CHILDREN'S DAY IN THE PARK
Enjoy food and activities for children of all ages. Location: Johnson Park

APRIL 26
CITYWIDE GARAGE SALE
More than 50 different garage sales in one location, 9:00 am to 4:00 pm. Location: Johnson Park

MAY 8-11
MAYFEST
Carnival, washer pitching & volleyball tournaments, parade, bathtub races, barbeque cook-off, Womanless Style Show, live music, arts, crafts & food vendors, and a ton of family fun.

JULY 4
INDEPENDENCE DAY CELEBRATION
PATRIOTIC
For the family, bands play and fireworks at dusk. Location: Lakeside Park

AUGUST 8-10
LAKEFEST DRAG BOAT RACE
More than 100 boats on a liquid quarter-mile racing at speeds up to 200 mph. Location: Lakeside Park & Johnson Park

SEPTEMBER 13
MARKET DAY
More than 100 vendors with a variety of items, 9:00 am to 4:00 pm. Location: Main Street

OCTOBER 4
CITYWIDE GARAGE SALE
More than 50 different garage sales in one location, 9:00 am to 4:00 pm. Location: Johnson Park

OCTOBER 30-31
MOONLIGHT MADNESS

NOVEMBER 1-2
ANTIQUES & COLLECTIBLES SHOW
In conjunction with Show-N-Shine Car Show on Main Street, individuals and local businesses gather to sell a variety of antiques and collectibles. Location: Lakeside Pavilion

TEXAS HILL COUNTRY WINERIES SPECIAL EVENTS! PLEASE VISIT WWW.TEXASWINETRAIL.COM FOR MORE INFORMATION!

WINE LOVERS TRAIL
FEB 8-10 & 15-17

WINE AND WILDFLOWER TRAIL
APR 4-6 & 11-13

HARVEST WINE TRAIL
AUG 1-3 & 8-10

TEXAS WINE MONTH TRAIL
OCT. 1-31ST

HOLIDAY WINE TRAIL
DEC 5-7 & DEC 12-14

We hope you join us... for a weekend or a lifetime
Visitor Center located in the old train depot at 801 Hwy 281
800-759-8178 www.marblefalls.org

marblefalls/lakelbj
chamber of commerce